Dún Laoghaire-Rathdown
County Council Comhairle Contae
Dhún Laoghaire-Ráth an Dúin

www.dlrcoco.ie/library

Public Library Service
Seirbhís Leabharlainne Poiblí

**Dún Laoghaire
Library
Tel: 2801254**

821

– *Items to be returned on or before the last date below.*
– *Tá na hearraí le tabhairt ar ais ar, nó roimh, an dáta
deireanach atá thíosluaite.*

12 AUG 08

12 MAR 09

03 JAN 09
15/1/09

D1612780

LAUGH AT GILDED BUTTERFLIES

LAUGH AT
GILDED BUTTERFLIES

… so we'll live,
And pray, and sing, and tell old tales,
*   and laugh*
At gilded butterflies …

Ulick O'Connor

The Liffey Press

Published by
The Liffey Press
Ashbrook House 10 Main Street
Raheny, Dublin 5, Ireland
www.theliffeypress.com

Anthology © 2007 by Ulick O'Connor

A catalogue record of this book is
available from the British Library.

ISBN 978-1-905785-35-3

Printed in the UK by Athenaeum Press

CONTENTS

vii

INTRODUCTION

Two years ago I published a selection of poems from a weekly column of mine in the *Evening Herald* in which I choose a poem and explain to the reader why it appeals to me. This first volume has sold out, so I now feel that a selection from poems which have appeared in the column since then may once more appeal to readers.

Terry Wogan was kind enough to say in his foreword to the previous volume that

> 'With his eye for beauty, and his love of words
> Ulick O'Connor has selected well for your delight.'

I hope that once again in *Laugh at Gilded Butterflies* readers may experience the delight that a true poem can bring before the mind's eye.

Acknowledgements

I would like to acknowledge the help of my assistant Anna Harrison in the compiling of this volume, and the sympathy and encouragement of the staff of the *Evening Herald* who present my Rhyme and Reason poetry column. Also Jennifer Ryan, researcher, and Charlotte Bruton of The Marsh Agency, London.

Ulick O'Connor
November 2007

To AJF who has erected a chapel in honour of
Gerard Manley Hopkins

LEAR:
No, no, no, no! Come, let's away to prison;
We two alone will sing like birds i' the cage:
When thou dost ask me blessing, I'll kneel down,
And ask of thee forgiveness: so we'll live,
And pray, and sing, and tell old tales, and laugh
At gilded butterflies, and hear poor rogues
Talk of court news; and we'll talk with them too,
Who loses and who wins; who's in, who's out;
And take upon's the mystery of things,
As if we were God's spies: and we'll wear out,
In a wall'd prison, packs and sets of great ones
That ebb and flow by the moon.

William Shakespeare
King Lear, Act V, Scene III

MATTHEW ARNOLD
1822-1888

The sea of faith is on the ebb, organised religion is under threat. Matthew Arnold, the English poet, deplored a similar decline in the Victorian England, which his father, as head-master of Rugby School, had helped to shape. But it would take two world wars before the poem 'Dover Beach', in which Arnold prophetically wrote about England's loss of faith, could be applicable on a world scale including our own sainted isle. In 1933 Yeats would write 'The Second Coming' in anticipation of an apocalypse, which would descend as a result of mankind's misuse of the forces of nature. Despite his intense Englishness, Arnold had a soft spot for the Irish and he was the first to demonstrate that Shakespeare's, Byron's and Keats's genius derived from the 'natural magic' of their Celtic roots and not the hoarse vowels of the now discredited Anglo-Saxon *Beowulf*. I thought it not inappropriate then to begin this selection with 'Dover Beach' by Matthew Arnold and end it with Yeats's 'The Second Coming'.

from Dover Beach

The sea is calm to-night,
The tide is full, the moon lies fair
Upon the straits; – on the French coast, the light
Gleams, and is gone; the cliffs of England stand,
Glimmering and vast, out in the tranquil bay.
Come to the window, sweet is the night air!
Only, form the long line of spray
Where the ebb meets the moon-blanch'd sand,
Listen! you hear the grating roar
Of pebbles which the waves suck back, and fling,
At their return, up the high strand,
Begin, and cease, and then again begin,
With tremulous cadence slow, and bring
The eternal note of sadness in.
...   .

The sea of faith
Was once, too, at the full, and round earth's shore
Lay like the folds of a bright girdle furl'd;
But now I only hear
Its melancholy, long, withdrawing roar,
Retreating to the breath
Of the night-wind down the vast edges drear
And naked shingles of the world.

Ah, love, let us be true
To one another! For the world, which seems
To lie before us like a land of dreams,
So various, so beautiful, so new,
Hath really neither joy, nor love, nor light
Nor certitude, nor peace, nor help for pain;
And we are here as on a darkling plain.

3

PATRICK KAVANAGH
1905-1967

April showers may bring forth May flowers. But the only flower that dares to show its head in harsh March is the nodding daffodil. Patrick Kavanagh though was a fan of March. He felt himself fondled by its sleety winds and admired the sun fighting to survive in the torn sky.

Shancoduff is an astonishing poem to have written at the age of twenty-six on a small Monaghan farm. It would be hard to beat 'the bright shillings of March'. He and Yeats, I think, are our two finest poets of the century.

Kavanagh himself wrote about this poem: 'Curious this, how I had started off with the right simplicity, indifferent to crude reason and then ploughed my way through complexities and anger, hatred and ill-will towards the faults of man and came back to where I started.'

Shancoduff

My black hills have never seen the sun rising,
Eternally they look north towards Armagh.
Lot's wife would not be salt if she had been
Incurious as my black hills that are happy
When dawn whitens Glassdrummond chapel.

My hills hoard the bright shillings of March
While the sun searches in every pocket.
They are my Alps and I have climbed the Matterhorn
With a sheaf of hay for three perishing calves
In the field under the Big Forth of Rocksavage.

The sleety winds fondle the rushy beards of Shancoduff
While the cattle-drovers sheltering in the Featherna Bush
Look up and say: 'Who owns them hungry hills
That the water-hen and snipe must have forsaken?
A poet? Then by heavens he must be poor.'
I hear and is my heart not badly shaken?

W.B. YEATS
1866-1939

Though he had written in his youth of the dangers inherent
for a poet in love, Yeats had a number of beautiful lovers:
Dorothy Wellesley, Olivia Shakespeare and Ethel Mannin.
Then, when he was in his seventies, an exquisite twenty-year-
old Margot Ruddock fascinated him by the way she could
move from speech to song.

> 'All famine struck I, and then
> Those generous eyes on mine were cast'

This was opposite to what he had thought in his youth when
he wrote the beautiful 'Never Give all the Heart' after his fail-
ure to win Maud Gonne.

Never Give All the Heart

Never give all the heart, for love
Will hardly seem worth thinking of
To passionate women if it seem
Certain, and they never dream
That it fades out from kiss to kiss;
For everything that's lovely is
But a brief, dreamy, kind delight.
O never give the heart outright,
For they, for all smooth lips can say,
Have given their hearts up to the play.
And who could play it well enough
If deaf and dumb and blind with love?
He that made this knows all the cost,
For he gave all his heart and lost.

HILAIRE BELLOC
1870-1953

George Bernard Shaw used say about his literary rival Hilaire Belloc that he had 'prodigious gifts but is wasting them in the service of the Pope. If he must have a Pope there is quite possibly one in myself.'

Belloc represented the muscular Christianity of his day and used to engage in public confrontations with Shaw which drew huge crowds akin to the way pop groups do today. Between indulging in politics on the Christian Front, however, and undertaking ferocious journeys to write his famous travel books, Belloc tended to neglect the art he was best at – that of writing poetry. The sonnet below addressed to sleep has a high place in the English literary calendar. It is almost as if we are on board a boat sailing softly into a benevolent night before blessed oblivion settles in.

Shakespeare has always been thought to have had the last word on that exquisite moment before we join with sister sleep with 'Sleep that knits up the ravelled sleeve of care'. But I think old Hilary (as his friends used to call him) in this sonnet brings us as close as any poet has done to that unconscious state in which we spend one-quarter of our lives.

To Sleep

O my companion, O my sister Sleep,
The valley is all before us, bear me on.
High through the heaven of evening, hardly gone,
Beyond the harbour lights, beyond the sleep,
Beyond the land and its lost benison
To where, majestic on the darkening deep,
The night comes forward from mount Aurion.
O my companion, O my sister Sleep.

Above the surf-line, into the night-breeze;
Eastward above the ever-whispering seas;
Through the warm airs with no more watch to keep.
My day's run out and all its dooms are graven.
O dear forerunner of Death and promise of Haven.
O my companion, O my sister Sleep.

SEAMUS HEANEY
1939–

Early Irish folklore thrills with birdsong. The Irish god of love, Aengus, was said to have had a rosary of birds singing about his head as he walked along. The monk in his cell tuned in as he took up his quill for his morning task and let the music wander through his words as they emerged on the page. The flight of the swallows to the south is woven into Irish verse from Yeats and Wilde to Ledwidge, so it is not surprising that Seamus Heaney, our latest Nobel Prize winner, should have written this perfect piece about the little creatures.

St. Francis and the Birds

When Francis preached love to the birds,
They listened, fluttered, throttled up
Into the blue like a flock of words

Released for fun from his holy lips.
Then wheeled back, whirred about his head,
Pirouetted on brothers' capes,

Danced on the wing, for sheer joy played
And sang, like images took flight.
Which was the best poem Francis made,

His argument true, his tone light.

A.E. HOUSMAN
1859-1936

Though A.E. Housman is still one of the most widely read poets, for some reason the seventieth anniversary of his death seemed to pass almost unnoticed. He wrote just three books of fine verse to which the Shropshire hills form a backdrop. Mind you, there was a twenty-six year gap between the fabulous success of his first book, *A Shropshire Lad*, and the last one he published, *Last Poems*. It's rather comforting to know that he failed his degree at Oxford and then went on to become a noted classical scholar at Cambridge whose critical edition of *Juvenal* is still in use today.

Housman was a buttoned-up gay whose emotions brimmed over into exquisite evocations of nature, such as this one of the delightful spectacle we could be seeing below one of these days, if that filthy north-eastern wind would relax its month-long whip.

Loveliest of Trees

Loveliest of trees, the cherry now
Is hung with bloom along the bough,
And stands about the woodland ride
Wearing white for Eastertide.

Now, of my three score years and ten,
Twenty will not come again,
And take from seventy springs a score,
It only leaves me fifty more.

And since to look at things in bloom
Fifty springs are little room,
About the woodlands I will go
To see the cherry hung with snow.

GEORGE GORDON, LORD BYRON
1788-1824

I so like Byron's poetry. Born into the aristocracy, George Gordon, Lord Byron was crippled from birth with a twisted left leg. This didn't stop him from being opening bat for Harrow, and one of two students who jumped up the steps at Trinity College, Cambridge in one leap (this was relayed to me by Bob Tisdall, Ireland's Olympic gold medallist who also performed this feat.)

Byron died for freedom. He went to battle when the Greeks were attacked by the Turks and was killed in 1824 aged thirty-six. How could he have pushed himself in to writing such a vast volume of poetry in such a short span, it is impossible to say. How often his poems offer a balm to reader's minds when they ponder the mystery of broken love?

from When We Two Parted

When we two parted
In silence and tears,
Half broken-hearted,
To sever for years,
Pale grew thy cheek and cold,
Colder thy kiss;
Truly that hour foretold
Sorrow to this!

The dew of the morning
Sunk chill on my brow;
It felt like the warning
Of what I feel now.
Thy vows are all broken,
And light is thy fame:
I hear thy name spoken
And share in its shame.

In secret we met:
In silence I grieve
That thy heart could forget,
Thy spirit deceive.
If I should meet thee
After long years,
How should I greet thee?-
With silence and tears.

J.O. WALLIN
1779-1839

Dublin (originally Dyfflin), Cork and Limerick were founded by Scandinavians. In no other counties will you see as many people with the Irish combination of green eyes and red hair. I came across an eighteenth-century poem by a Swedish archbishop which, from the way it deals with the union of God and nature, could have been written by a ninth-century Irish monk in his cell. I translated it into English and the hymn was later sung by a school choir, under Isabel McCarthy, at St. Nicholas Church of Ireland in Dundalk in a service conducted by that splendid man, the late Archbishop George Simms. Well here it is. Is there not a whiff somewhere in it of St. Kevin and his singing birds of Glendalough?

Where is the Friend

Where is the Friend that everywhere I'm seeking?
When daylight comes my longing grows for Thee, King.
When day departs I have not found my Master,
Though the heart beats faster.

I hear his Voice where summer winds are breathing,
Where forests sing, and where the river's seething.
Its splendour fills me, and where that Voice is,
My heart rejoices.

I sense his Being in every move of nature,
The flower that blooms, and bends towards its Creator,
The very air I breathe, each sigh I utter,
Mingles with my Lover

Be strong my soul, hope, pray, surrender.
Your friend beckons: soon you'll taste how tender
His love can be; and sink upon his Bosom
And never lose Him.

(Translated by Ulick O'Connor)

D.H. LAWRENCE
1885-1930

With the loosening of the censorship laws these days it's hard to remind ourselves that it's only three decades or so that D.H. Lawrence's *Lady Chatterley's Lover* was unbanned in the US and Britain. Brendan Behan remarked at the time that if the title had been changed to *Slattery's Mounted Slut* (a play on the ballad *Slattery's Mounted Foot*) it might have been unbanned here as well.

In fact, read today *Lady Chatterley* exudes a spiritual element characteristic of D.H. Lawrence's mystical view of life. But the narrow-eyed censor couldn't see through the grimy bits to the shining light behind. Here's how the alleged pornographer David H. Lawrence exquisitely defines the relationship between God and man.

from The Hands of God

It is a fearful thing to fall into the hands of the living
  God
But it is a much more fearful thing to fall out of them.

Did Lucifer fall through knowledge?
O then pity him, pity him that plunge!

Save me, O God, from falling into the ungodly
  knowledge
of myself as I am without God.
Let me never know, O God
let me never know what I am or should be
when I have fallen out of your hands, the hands of
  the living God
    ...   .

Save me, from that O God!
Let me never know myself apart from the living God!

19

LYNN C. DOYLE
1873-1961

The repeated Westminster elections have emphasised the depth of tribal division in Northern Ireland. We shouldn't forget though that under the mask of Orangeman and Papist there is a personality special to Ulstermen no matter what side they come from. Someone who spotted this better than most was a County Down Protestant, Lynn Doyle, who had come to live in Dublin between the two wars. He had become famous in Dublin as author of most of the witty remarks that were circulating the town at that time. It was he who described the difference between the then Gate Theatre and the Abbey as that of 'Sodom and Begorrah'. When asked how he would like to celebrate the fiftieth anniversary of his marriage he replied, 'Three minutes' silence'. As a newly-appointed film censor he explained to the press that his job was to 'stop the californication of Ireland'.

But it was when he became one of the best-read Irish novelists of his time with his stories of Ulster farm folk in a mythical village called Ballygullion that his skill in discerning the humour and kindness under the dour exterior of the Ulster Protestant was recognised. His real name was Leslie Alan Montgomery and he had taken his pseudonym Lynn. C. Doyle from a bottle which he saw in a village shop containing linseed oil. Here is his poem dealing with an Ulster farmer's grudging affection for his Catholic neighbour.

An Ulsterman

I do not like the other sort;
They're tricky an' they're sly,
An' couldn't look you in the face
Whenever they pass by.
Still I'll give in that here an' there,
You'll meet a decent man;
I would make an exception, now,
About wee Michael Dan.

A better neighbour couldn't be,
He borrows an' he lends;
An' – bar a while about the Twelfth
When him and me's not friends –
He'll never wait until he's asked
To lend a helpin' han'
There's quite a wheen of Protestants
I'd swop for Michael Dan.

So, while I have my private doubts
About him reachin' heaven,
His feet keeps purty near the pad
On six days out of seven;
An' if it falls within the scope
Of God Almighty's plan
To save a single Papish soul,
I hope it's Michael Dan.

Arthur Geoghegan
1810-1899

The middle of March is a time of celebration of both orange and green traditions. The white in the national flag is a symbol of the link between the two. The ludicrous fact is that when the Irish fought against William of Orange in 1691 they were doing so on behalf of an English king who was holding on to his throne against a Dutch usurper of base origins. After King James did a runner the Irish were led by the splendid Patrick Sarsfield whose country house in Lucan is today the residence of the Italian Ambassador. Sarsfield's last words as he lay dying at the battle of Landen in the Low Countries were, 'Oh that this were for Ireland'.

Nearly every Irish poet has had a shot at verse about the Wild Geese, those gallant Irish gentlemen who rather than serve under Orange Billy after Aughrim was lost went to France, Spain and Russia, where their military feats became legendary. Three marshals of European armies in the eighteenth century were Irish born: Maximilian Ulysses Brown, Austria; Peter Lally, Russia; and Lord Clare, France.

Willie Yeats and Emily Lawless top the list for wild goosery, a close runner up is a Dublin civil servant Arthur Gerald Geoghegan, who wrote the exquisite little piece below. Geoghegan died in London in 1899.

After Aughrim

Do you remember long ago, Kathaleen?
When your lover whispered low,
'Shall I stay or shall I go, Kathaleen?'
And you answered proudly, 'Go!
And join King James and strike a blow
For the Green.'

Mavrone, your hair is white as snow, Kathaleen;
Your heart is sad and full of woe,
Do you repent you made him go, Kathaleen
And quick you answer proudly, 'No!
For better die with Sarsfield so,
Than live a slave without a blow
For the Green.'

THOMAS DAVIS
1814-1845

Recently Thomas Davis's 'A Nation Once Again', written more than 150 years ago, won a European song prize. In 1922 it was expected to have been chosen as the Irish national anthem but because of Civil War politics 'A Soldier's Song' was chosen instead as it had been the marching song of the Volunteers during the War of Independence.

Davis's influence on Irish history is enormous but underestimated. He died at the age of thirty-one of scarlatina. But the writers of his paper *The Nation* would be the source of much of the thinking behind Irish politics in the next fifty years, especially Griffith, Pearse and De Valera.

Davis's songs, 'The West's Asleep', 'The Girl I Left Behind Me', 'Eibhlin a Rúin' were sung throughout the country. He was in particular a great admirer of the Wild Geese, those 400,000 Irishman who after the defeat by the Orange King of England at Limerick went into exile and became famous among the armies of France, Austria and Russia for their military skill. The greatest victory of the Irish Brigade was at the battle of Fontenoy in 1745 when Louis XIV was being driven back by the English and called in his Irish left flank to confront the British guards. The Irish not only won the battle but seized the guards' colours of the Brigade and brought them back to Paris where they were hung in Les Invalides. Here is how Davis imagines the scene in the mess tent of the brigade the night before the exiles set out for the fray.

The Battle Eve of the Brigade

The mess-tent is full, and the glasses are set,
And the gallant Count Thomond is president yet;
The vet'ran arose, like an uplifted lance,
Crying – 'Comrades, a health to the monarch of France!'
With bumpers and cheers they have done as he bade,
For King Louis is loved by the Irish Brigade.

'A health to King James,' and they bent as they quaffed,
'Here's to Georgie the Dutchman,' and fiercely they
      laughed
'Good luck to the girls we wooed long ago,
Where Shannon, and Barrow, and Blackwater flow;'
'God prosper Old Ireland' – you'd think them afraid,
So pale grew the chiefs of the Irish Brigade.

'But surely, that light cannot be from our lamp
And that noise – are they all getting drunk in the camp?'
'Hurrah! Boys, the morning of battle is come,
And the generale's beating on many a drum.'
So they rush from the revel to join the parade:
For the van is the right of the Irish Brigade.

They fought as they revelled, fast, fiery and true,
And, though victors, they left on the field not a few;
And they, who survived, fought and drank as of yore
But the land of their heart's hope they never saw more;
For in far foreign fields, from Dunkirk to Belgrade,
Lie the soldiers and chiefs of the Irish Brigade.

EDWARD THOMAS
1878-1917

On Easter Day ninety years ago the poet Edward Thomas was killed in action at the Battle of Arras. Though he is remembered among England's dazzling array of war poets, the extraordinary thing is he hadn't begun to write poetry until three years before his death at the age of thirty-nine. Until 1914 he had made his living as a biographer and writer of reviews. But encouraged by Robert Frost, the American poet, he began to write poetry, which was to have a real influence on the course of English verse. With a poet's natural ear he was able to take everyday words and make them glow as he fitted them into rhythms which were running through his mind. So subtle was his craft that sometimes you have to read his verse a number of times before you hear the inner music.

One writer influenced by Thomas' innovations was Philip Larkin, the finest English poet of the second half of the twentieth century. The poem below, 'Like the Touch of Rain', should be spoken out loud and about the third or fourth time you should get the tune. By the way, his real name was Edward Eastaway. No wonder he changed his moniker!

Like the Touch of Rain

Like the touch of rain she was
On a man's flesh and hair and eyes
When the joy of walking thus
Has taken him by surprise:

With the love of the storm he burns,
He sings, he laughs, well I know how,
But forgets when he returns
As I shall not forget her 'Go now'.

Those two words shut a door
Between me and the blessed rain
That was never shut before
And will not open again.

ELEANOR HULL
1860-1935

Not many people, when they are singing in church one of the most famous hymns in the world, 'Be Thou My Vision', know that it was written by an Irish lady named Eleanor Hull. She took the words from an old Gaelic poem which she adapted to the music from an Irish folk song 'Slane', written about the hill where St. Patrick lit candles on Easter eve. Eleanor Hull was educated at Dublin's Alexandra College and later founded the important Irish Texts Society, which carried on the work begun by Oscar Wilde's mother, Lady Wilde, in collecting the unique oral literature that was still alive on the lips of the country people in the nineteenth century.

One poem discovered and translated by Eleanor Hull could have been written today, so aptly does it catch the angst generated by *le jeux d'amour* – love's little game.

from Love is a Mortal Disease

My grief and my pain! A mortal disease is love,
Woe, woe unto him who must prove it a month or even a
    day,
It hath broken my heart, and my bosom is burdened
    with sighs,
From dreaming of her, gentle sleep hath forsaken mine
    eyes.

It seems to me long till the tide washes up on the strand;
It seems to me long till the night shall fade into day;
It seems to me long till the cocks crow on every hand;
And rather than the world were I close beside my love.

My woe and my plight! Where tonight is the snowdrift
    and frost?
Or even I and my love together breasting the waves of
    the sea;
Without bark, without boat, without any vessel with me,
But I to be swimming, and my arm to be circling his
    waist!

(circa early seventeenth century)

EDGAR ALLEN POE
1809-1849

It was an American poet of an Irish Catholic background who exercised a powerful influence on French literature in the nineteenth century. Baudelaire, Mallarmé and Verlaine took considerable chunks of their poetic philosophy from Edgar Allen Poe's long poem 'The Raven'. Though the poor man died at forty (he was fond of the drink), he remains famous in literature today for his novels *The Murder in the Room Morgue* (the first modern detective story) and *The Fall of the House of Usher*. These horror novels have, to some extent, blinded readers to the beautiful love lyrics he wrote which could have come from the lute of an Italian troubadour. Every good anthology contains either one or other of his two most famous poems, 'To Helen' or 'Annabel Lee'.

from Annabel Lee

It was many and many a year ago,
In a kingdom by the sea,
That a maiden there lived whom you may know
By the name of Annabel Lee.
And this maiden she lived with no other thought
Than to loved and be loved by me.

I was a child and she was a child
In this kingdom by the sea:
But we loved with a love that was more than love –
I and my Annabel Lee,
With a love that the winged seraphs of heaven
Coveted her and me.

And this was the reason that, long ago,
In this kingdom by the sea,
A wind blew out of a cloud, chilling
My beautiful Annabel Lee,
So that her high-born kinsman came
And bore her away from me,
To shut her up in a sepulchere
In this kingdom by the sea.

And so, all the night-tide, I lie down by the side
Of my darling – my darling – my life and my bride,
In the sepulcher there by the sea,
In her tomb by the sounding sea.

D.H. LAWRENCE
1885-1930

With a magnificent Yeats exhibition in the National Library, and another last year for Joyce, one wonders why the only other writer in their class in English, D.H. Lawrence, has had so little attention in his own country. Maybe, despite all they say, we value our writers more here.

Of course, D.H. Lawrence is associated with the scandal of *Lady Chatterley's Lover*, considered too obscene for English readers until 1961, and controversy surrounded some of his other novels. But nothing can conceal the splendid humanity of *Sons and Lovers*, his novel about himself and his mother, and there is a tendency, too, to forget that his collected poems are twice as big as Yeats's and make Joyce's *Chamber Music* look like a leaflet. Here is a Lawrence piece, 'Piano', which one feels that W.B. or James of the Joyces himself would not have disdained to have attributed to them.

Piano

Softly, in the dusk, a woman is singing to me;
Taking me back down the vista for years, till I see
A child sitting under the piano, in the boom of the
    tingling strings
And pressing the small, poised feet of a mother who
    smiles as she sings.

In spite of myself, the insidious mastery of song
Betrays me back, till the heart of me weeps to belong
To the old Sunday evenings at home, with winter outside
And hymns in the cosy parlour, the tinkling piano our
    guide.

So now it is vain for the singer to burst into clamour
With the great black piano appassionato. The glamour
Of childish days is upon me, my manhood is cast
Down in the flood of remembrance, I weep like a child
    for the past.

Philip Larkin
1922-1985

Aubade is defined as a musical announcement of dawn. You'd need it these days when we wake up shanghaied by the schedules we set out for ourselves. Philip Larkin, England's greatest modern poet, was no fan of morning music. He hated those hours when light began to usurp the dark. He was devoted to his mother and after she died the light seemed to creep in the window in the morning with a different tint. Then religion went from him:

> 'That vast moth-eaten musical brocade
> Created to pretend we never die'

He was also keeping three lovers at the one time (without any knowing of the others) which put a strain on his stamina.

This somewhat hair-raising poem confronts a future faced without the crutch of religion.

from Aubade

I work all day, and get half-drunk at night.
Waking at four to soundless dark, I stare.
In time the curtain-edges will grow light.
Till then I see what's really always there:
Unresting death, a whole day nearer now,
Making all thought impossible but how
And where and when I shall myself die.
Arid interrogation: yet the dread
Of dying, and being dead,
Flashes afresh to hold and horrify.

...   .

This is a special way of being afraid
No trick dispels. Religion used to try,
That vast, moth-eaten musical brocade
Created to pretend we never die,
And specious stuff that says No rational being
Can fear a thing it will not feel, not seeing
That this is what we fear - no sight, no sound,
No touch or taste or smell, nothing to think with,
Nothing to love or link with,
The anasthetic from which none come round

And so it stays just on the edge of vision,
A small, unfocused blur, a standing chill
That slows each impulse down to indecision.
Most things may never happen: this one will,
And realisation of it rages out
In furnace-fear when we are caught without
People or drink. Courage is no good:
It means not scaring others. Being brave

Lets no one off the grave.
Death is no different whined at than withstood.

Slowly light strengthens, and the room takes shape.
It stands plain as a wardrobe, what we know,
Have always known, know that we can't escape,
Yet can't accept. One side will have to go.
Meanwhile telephones crouch, getting ready to ring
In locked-up offices, and all the uncaring
Intricate rented world begins to rouse.
The sky is white as clay, with no sun.
Work has to be done
Postmen like doctors go from house to house.

CHRISTY BROWN
1932-1981

This year is the seventy-fifth anniversary of Christy Brown's birth and there has hardly been a whisper about him. Yet in many ways Christy was one of the most outstanding writers of our time. Born a little quivering mass of inarticulate flesh, the medical diagnosis was that the child was unlikely to communicate with the outside world. But boy did he!

He was to write one of the unique novels of the first half of the century, *Down All the Days*, which has been translated into thirteen languages. Christy was also a splendid painter and had a short-term wit that could stiffen a serpent's eyebrows. He achieved world fame despite the fact that because of his cerebral palsy his painting and writing had to be done with brush or pen held in his left foot. His halting speech didn't impede a rapier wit. I opened one of his first painting exhibitions for him. He was sitting in his wheelchair beside me. I referred to the fact that if his mother had been alive she would have been so proud of him. He plucked my arm. 'She is here', he said firmly, and for a moment the room flooded with her presence.

Born in Stannaway Road, only a few hundred yards from where Brendan Behan was born, Christy was an inherent part of the Behan, O'Casey, James Plunkett world-class writing geniuses that Dublin produced, who made an impression throughout the world. His mother ran the household like an efficient republic. Each member had a function to undertake. She had borne twenty-three children of whom thirteen survived. To have nursed, in such circumstances, an incapacitated child into a world genius was extraordinary. It was after her death that Christy married, and inexplicably went to live

37

in Kerry (of all places) and finally to Somerset. He proved un-receptive to both Kerry *plamás* and English taciturnity, and in exile his talent diminished. But to most of his early work there is no other word one could apply except genius. Many great poems have been written by sons to their mothers, but Christy Brown's must rank among the finest of them all. It has a courtly Elizabethan style combined with the visceral love that Dublin mothers like Kathleen Behan and Susan O'Casey held for their children.

from For My Mother

Only in your dying, Lady, could I offer you a poem.

Never in life could I capture that free live spirit of a girl
in the torn and tattered net of my words
Your life was a buried flower
burning on an ash-heap.

You were a song inside my skin
a sudden sunburst of defiant laughter
spilling over the night-gloom of my half awakenings
a firefly of far splendid light
dancing in the dim catacombs of my brain

Only in your dying Lady, could I offer you a poem.

With gay uplifted finger you beckoned
and faltering I followed you down paths
I would not otherwise have known or dared.

Only in dying, Lady, could I offer you a poem.

I do not grieve for you
in your little square plot of indiscriminate clay
for now shall you truly dance.

MRS. FRANCES ALEXANDER
1818-1895

Perhaps the hymn most sung in the English speaking world today is the lovely 'All Things Bright and Beautiful'. It was written by a Wicklow woman, Frances Alexander, who also wrote another world famous hymn, 'There is a Green Hill Far Away'. Strangely enough, number three in the list of fine hymns of the nineteenth century is by Irish scholar and poet Eleanor Hull, and is a translation of a ninth-century Gaelic poem 'Be Thou My Vision, O Lord of My Heart'. These all came from the Church of Ireland community. What's sad is that beautiful hymns in English sung in Catholic churches up to forty years ago have now been booted out by an ignorant junta so that you are as likely these days to hear wild guitar playing and something approaching rap, emanating from the choir loft.

Frances Alexander's husband, by the way, was Protestant Archbishop of All Ireland. He was also a famous preacher, though he had a problem whenever he had to speak from the pulpit of the Chapel Royal in Dublin Castle. The entrance to the pulpit was awkwardly arranged with a narrow stair leading to it and as he was a colossal mountain of a man three little choir boys had to get behind him like the back row of a rugby scrum to push him up to his perch. The effort was worth it for his voice and eloquence were apparently mighty.

All Things Bright and Beautiful

All things bright and beautiful,
All creatures great and small,
All things wise and wonderful,
The Lord God made them all.

Each little flower that opens,
Each little bird that sings,
He made their glowing colours,
He made their tiny wings.

The purple-headed mountain,
The river running by,
The sunset, and the morning,
That brightens up the sky;

He gave us eyes to see them,
And lips that we might tell,
How great is God Almighty,
Who has made all things well.

JULIAN GRENFELL
1885-1915

On Remembrance Day poppies are worn to commemorate those who died in the First World War. Fifty thousand nationalist Irishmen who believed they were fighting for Home Rule died in that war and got nothing back in return. Most of those taking part thought they were fighting for freedom, when it was really a battle between market forces as to who would control finance in the twentieth century.

We should remember, however, that a large section of the English population was deceived as well, and it wasn't only the working class who were taken for a ride. High-minded people from the upper classes who had socialist instincts went out to fight for King and Crown without knowing that they were really fighting for the half-crown. Among them were two young aristocrats, Julian and Billy Grenfell, sons of Lord Desborough, who volunteered to fight immediately when the war broke out. They, and others, saw the battle as a sort of cleansing influence to rescue them from the shame of belonging to a class who had exploited those below them. The Honourable Julian Grenfell was said to be the handsomest young man in England before he was killed in the second year of the War. He was also a poet and here is his take on the fighting lark.

from Into Battle

The naked earth is warm with spring,
And with green grass and bursting trees
Leans to the sun's gaze glorying,
And quivers in the sunny breeze;
And life is colour and warmth and light,
And a striving evermore for these;
And he is dead who will not fight;
And who dies fighting has increase.

All the bright company of Heaven
Hold him in their high comradeship,
The Dog-Star, and the Sisters Seven,
Orion's Belt and sworded hip.

....

The thundering line of battle stands,
And in the air death moans and sings;
But Day shall clasp him with strong hands,
And Night shall fold him in soft wings.

FRANCIS MAHONY ('FATHER PROUT')
1805-1866

Cork man, Jesuit and dedicated hater, the Reverend Francis Mahony (who wrote under the name of Father Prout) has a poem, 'The Bells of Shandon', included in the *Oxford Book of English Verse* alongside the likes of Shakespeare, Keats, Thackeray and Yeats.

How was it done?

The fact is, to write a real poem is a sort of miracle. Some people do it once and never again, hit the magic button. Father Prout's poem, 'The Bells of Shandon', resounds with the sort of word music that Yeats achieves in 'The Lake Isle of Innisfree'. That Prout set out to achieve this we know from his own words: 'I wanted to produce, as Victor Hugo did when he clapped the Hunchback athwart the bells of Notre Dame in rapid succession, a musical roar, something more gladdening, more dazzling, more tumultuous; a storm of bells, a furnace of campanology, something that would even distantly imitate, in the language of the great romance itself, ten thousand brazen tones breathed all at once, from flute of stone three hundred high!'

Francis Mahony never renounced Holy Orders and said his office every day, but that was the extent of his priestly activities. He became a famous newspaper correspondent for the *London Daily News*, first in Rome and then in Paris. A collection of his newspaper writings is still in print, *The Reliques of Father Prout*. His best friend was William Thackeray, the famous English poet, and although they abused one another through the post for years, they remained close until the Cork man died at the age of sixty-one. He is buried at Shandon church in Cork.

from The Bells of Shandon

With deep affection and recollection
I often think of the Shandon bells,
Whose sounds so wild would, in days of childhood,
Fling round my cradle their magic spells.
On this I ponder, where'er I wander,
And thus grow fonder, sweet Cork, of thee,
With thy bells of Shandon,
That sound so grand on
The pleasant waters of the river Lee.
….. ….. …….. ….. ….. …..

I have heard bells tolling "old Adrian's mole" in,
Their thunder rolling from the Vatican,
With cymbals glorious, swinging uproarious
In the gorgeous turrets of Notre Dame;
But thy sounds were sweeter than the dome of Peter
Flings o'er the Tiber, pealing solemnly.
Oh! the bells of Shandon
Sound far more grand on
The pleasant waters of the River Lee.
…. … … … … …

45

JOHN PHILPOT CURRAN
1750-1817

The centenary of Robert Emmet, the Irish revolutionary, has brought his name before us yet again. Here is a verse by the patriot lawyer John Philpot Curran, the father of the love of Emmet's life, Sarah Curran. The only mark against Curran, the most famous orator of his time, is that he ordered his daughter out of his Rathfarnham house because of her love for Emmet.

Curran was himself an Irish patriot who after the rebellion of 1798 defended Wolfe Tone and used his oratory in memorable speeches against the Act of Union with England, which would bring Ireland once more under foreign rule. Curran was regarded as one of the wittiest men in Dublin and London, and his reply to the hanging judge Lord Norbury is still quoted at dinners in the Inns of Court: 'Is this meat well hung?' Norbury had said to Curran at dinner. 'It will be after your lordship has tried it.'

Curran understood Irish, and the Gaelic tradition of internal rhythm is used with great skill in this fine drinking song.

The Deserter's Meditation

If sadly thinking, with spirits sinking,
Could more than drinking my cares compose,
A cure for sorrow from sighs I'd borrow,
And hope to-morrow would end my woes.

But as in wailing there's nought availing,
And Death unfailing will strike the blow,
Then for that reason, and for a season,
Let us be merry before we go.

THOMAS MOORE
1779-1852

Little Tommy Moore, the grocer's son from 12 Aungier Street, achieved success as a poet in England that was never equalled by any other writer before or after him. He was paid the equivalent of half a million euro in advance for his long poem 'Lalla Rookh' even before he had written a line of it.

Tom mesmerised London society with his songs at the piano which he sang like Bing Crosby, almost half spoken, and was influential enough to have persuaded the Duke of Wellington (a Meath man) to finally push through the Catholic Emancipation Act. After Lord Byron's death it was considered a compliment to him that his friend Moore should have consented to write the biography.

Idolised in his time by Edgar Allen Poe and Sir Walter Scott for his lyrical poems like 'Lough Derg' and 'At the Mid Hour of Night', little Tommy, whose best pal at Trinity College Dublin was Robert Emmet, could also put the boot in when he wanted to.

His poem 'The Petition of the Orangemen of Ireland' (1816) could have been written in the last decade or so when our Northern brethren had been causing more than their usual share of trouble in the summer season

from The Petition of the Orangemen of Ireland

To the people of England, the humble Petition
Of Ireland's disconsolate Orangemen, showing –
That sad, very sad, is our present condition;
Our jobbing all gone and our noble selves going;

That, forming one seventh, within a few fractions,
Of Ireland's seven millions of hot heads and hearts,
We hold it the basest of all base transactions
To keep us from murd'ring the other six parts:

That, relying on England, whose kindness already
So often has helped us to play this game o'er,
We have got our red coats and our carabines ready,
And wait but he word to show sport as before.

JEAN ELLIOT
1727-1805

That great writer Sean O' Faoláin, when asked about his pref-
erence in poetry, came up with a poem by an eighteenth-
century Scottish aristocrat Jean Elliot as one of his favourite
choices. Jean Eliot made her poem the same way Yeats cob-
bled together his 'Down by the Sally Gardens'. She took an
old folk song and re-arranged it with a poet's hand till it is
now part of every good anthology of English verse. It laments
the defeat of the Scottish army by the English in the Battle of
Flodden, a battle which need never have been fought as the
Scots had previously defeated the English at Bannockburn. It
is written in Lowlands Scots dialect (Lallans) which has be-
come familiar because of Robert Burns's use of it in his poems.
It says much for the evocative power of Scots dialect that we
can read these beautiful poems without getting irritated by an
occasional buckled word which now and then pops up like
the squeak of a broken shoe.

Lady Jean Elliot, a Jacobite supporter, was the third
daughter of Sir Gilbert Elliot, later Lord Monto, a member of
the Scottish judiciary.

from Flowers of the Forest

I've heard them lilting at our ewe-milking,
Lasses a' lilting before dawn o' day;
But now they are moaning on ilka green loaning,
The Flowers of the Forest are a' wede away.

Dool and wae for the order sent our lads to the Border!
The English, for ance, by guile wan the day;
The Flowers of the Forest, that fought aye the foremost,
The prime of our land, lie cauld in the clay.

We'll hear nae mair lilting at our ewe-milking;
Women and bairns are heartless and wae;
Sighing and moaning on ilka green loaning
The Flowers of the Forest are a' wede away.

OLIVER ST. JOHN GOGARTY
1878-1957

August means autumn, though recently the fatal tinge hasn't shown because of the heat wave. Starting with Keats there has hardly been a poet who hasn't written on this season. A favourite autumn poem of mine was written by a lad who had just left Clongowes Wood College in 1899 and who would later be hailed by Yeats as 'One of the great lyric poets of our age'. What is exciting about Gogarty's poem is that if you listen carefully to the run of the lines you may just get a sense of the leaves drifting down. Pretty good for a lad who had just left school, and who must have had to spend a lot of time on his bicycle to break the Irish record for twenty miles which he held. Incidentally, he used to keep himself from getting bored in the saddle by reciting Greek poetry, oodles of which he knew by heart.

Folia Caduca

Autumn, autumn the leaves are falling.
Earth who has given them gladly, receives.
Through the thick air they come at her calling
A generation of golden leaves.

The generations descend and winter;
Winter from withering who can withhold?
Deathward he calls them and they go thither;
Leaves like men change Earth into gold.

I look on men like leaves and I ponder
On a golden death that no longer grieves
Where is the leaf that would carry beyond her
The spendthrift gold of the fallen leaves.

ALICE MEYNELL
1847-1922

When the Poet Laureateship became vacant in 1913, the position should have gone to a woman. But in those pre-feminist days the Establishment would rather have awarded the post to a Piccadilly newsboy than have a lady Laureate. Besides being a fine poet, Alice was a real beauty who could have stepped out of a pre-Raphaelite painting. Coventry Patmore, a poet very much in fashion at the time, was in love with her and wrote a collection of love letters to her which are among the most famous in literature. George Meredith the novelist was another Alice fan.

She and her husband Wilfred lived in a big house at Greatham where they hospitably allowed young poetesses to settle down so that 'all seemed song and study mixed with laughing girls'. Alice Meynell saved one junkie poet from destruction – Francis Thompson, author of 'The Hound of Heaven', the greatest mystical poet in English of the nineteenth century who used to follow her around obediently like a faithful dog. Her poem here is a miracle of simplicity, the most ordinary words endowed with the gleam of verse so that a poem flowers there.

Maternity

One wept whose only child was dead,
New-born, ten years ago.
'Weep not; he is in bliss', they said.
She answered, 'Even so,

'Ten years ago was born in pain
A child, not now forlorn.
But oh, ten years ago, in vain,
A mother, a mother was born'.

SEUMAS O'SULLIVAN
1879-1958

In the 1950s at twilight you could see the lamplighter on his bicycle with his long pole with a hook on the end of it, turning on the street lamps. He didn't stop, but skilfully slid past each post flicking his pole at the switch like a magician flooding the street with light. We called him 'Leary the Lamplighter'. On special occasions he would reproduce the sound of a motor horn, screwing his lips like a grapefruit slice.

Seumas O'Sullivan, who took the Dublin Streets for his *mise-en-scène*, has commemorated them in verse. It is hard to imagine that the same man who wrote this gentle poem could have had a tongue like a hatchet in conversation. Once when he saw a manure cart pass under his window in Pembroke Road he remarked, 'I see the poet Patrick Kavanagh is changing house'. Though he liked Kavanagh and admired his poetry he couldn't restrain the Swiftian snap.

The Lamp Lighter

Here to the leisured side of life,
Remote from traffic, free from strife,
A cul-de-sac, a sanctuary
Where old quaint customs creep to die
And only ancient memories stir
At evening comes the lamplighter;
With measured style without a sound,
He treads the unalterable round,
Soundlessly touching one by one.
The waiting posts that stand to take
The faint blue bubbles in his wake!
And when the night begins to wane
He comes to take them back again
Before the chilly dawn can blight
The delicate frail buds of light.

FRANCIS STUART
1902-2000

Though Francis Stuart wrote two of the finest novels of the twentieth century, *Redemption* and *Black List Section H,* he is hardly remembered as a poet. His wife Iseult (Maud Gonne's daughter) thought him a better poet than prose writer. When I once asked Francis why he didn't write more poetry he said, 'perhaps I am addicted to prose'.

In his poem 'Night Pilot' he has left us the perfect metaphor for the artist's function, that of a pilot without radar plunging into the darkness to glimpse what is beyond. Certainly Yeats thought Stuart's poetry was the best of his contemporaries and remarked of his novel *The Coloured Dome* that it was 'more personally and beautifully written than any book of our generation'.

Despite Stuart's mystical vocation he was a good mixer and before the last war he, Samuel Beckett and Liam O'Flaherty (all over six feet tall) were well known in bars like Davy Byrnes, The Bailey and Jammets, as well as the Leopardstown and Punchestown racecourses. Francis died at the age of ninety-eight and was still writing poetry, and always ready to have a good afternoon's talk.

Isuelt once said to him: 'I am the willow rooted on the river bank and you are the black swan gliding past.'

Though a decade before he had thought of a Dublin resting place, he is buried today along with his favourite cat, Min, in Clare where his third wife, Finola, still lives. Despite Yeats's high opinion of him, Stuart was not uncritical of the old poet while recognising him as one of the truly greats.

Remembering Yeats

Shadow on shadow his mind
Raised a temple of thought
And his aging body, blind,
Burning with mortal breath,
Groped to the inner court
To hide itself from death.

We sat with our guests after the meal
As they talked of Yeats and sipped their wine
And I wondered would they ever go
Asunder the table I felt your heel
While they spoke high art and quoted a line
From the Purgatorio

Who was it had known all Dante once?
Any why – though why not – had he called me a dunce?

He was rather rhetorical
And chose the wrong buddies.
In his august presence my blood ran cool
And my mouth dried up.
But he had his passion
As have only the great ones.
Yeats, we drink to you
In your final solitude.

PEADAR KEARNEY
1883-1942

Brendan Behan as a lad used to get a lot of kudos out of the fact that his uncle Peadar wrote the Irish National Anthem. Peadar was his mother's brother and the Kearney family ran a prosperous shop near the centre of the city on the north side before going bankrupt and slipping into poverty.

Peadar Kearney wrote 'The Soldier's Song' rather quickly, and I have never thought it up to the standard of some of his other marvellous songs: 'Down in the Village', 'Whack Fol the Diddle', 'Down by the Glenside' and 'The Three-Coloured Ribbon'. He was Property Master in the Abbey Theatre and toured England with the company before he adopted the profession of house painter. Peadar Kearney fought in Jacob's factory under Thomas McDonagh in the Rising in 1916 and later in the War of Independence, and was interned in Ballykinlar camp. Brendan Behan may have got something of his wit from his uncle who remarked about Joyce's *Ulysses* when it was first published, 'It would be an excellent book for a theological student in a seminary because every possible mortal sin is mentioned in it'.

'The Three-Coloured Ribbon' is that rare product, a true ballad with the whiff of the street and a subtle rhythmic undertone which any poet could be proud of.

from **The Three-Coloured Ribbon**

I had a true love if ever a girl had one,
I had a true love, a brave lad was he,
One fine Easter Monday with his gallant comrades
He started away for to set old Ireland free.

All round my hat I wear a three-coloured ribbon
All round my hat until death comes to me,
And if anybody's asking me
Why do I wear it –
It's all for my true love I never more will see.

   ...   .

His bandolier round him, his bright bayonet shining;
His short service rifle, a beauty to see;
There was joy in his eyes tho' he left me behind him
And started away for to set Ireland free

ANTHONY RAFTERY
1784-1835

No poem has been more translated from Gaelic than Anthony Raftery's 'Killeaden'. It is the perfect poem of the poet's journey, always searching for the new, never content to rest on the reassurance of routine.

It was Douglas Hyde, our first president, who saved Raftery's work from extinction when he wrote his life and translated his poetry into English in 1893. Hyde had simply gone round the countryside with pen and notebook copying down from people the literary treasures that remained in their memory and which retained some of the exquisite traces of court verse. He had first heard of Raftery of all places in a Dublin street, when a beggar-man spoke to him in Irish and identified the house in Craughwell where Raftery had died. When Hyde visited that house the old woman who lived there said to him:'If it was music Raftery had chosen there would not have been another musician in the world as good as him. But he chose the talk. A voice like the wind he had.'

Frank O'Connor made a pretty good shot at translating the poem. Coslett Quinn and James Stephens were others who tried it. But my wreath for first place goes to Brendan Kennelly, who is one of the three best Irish poets we have writing in English today. There is a marvellous line in Brendan's translation in the third verse – 'My heart swells and lifts just like a rising tide' – which is a simply exquisite image of the lover's heart whenever the beloved hoves in sight, and at the same time conveys perfectly the inevitable progression of the elements.

County Mayo

Now with the Springtime there's a great stretch in the
  days
And after Brigid's feastday I'll Gather my traps and go,
Since I took it into my head, no chance that I'll delay
Till I find myself in the middle of the county Mayo.

In the town of Claremorris I'll spend the first gay night
And in Balla behind it I'll drink porter galore,
Then I'll hit for Kiltimagh and a full month's delight,
A bare two miles away from Ballinamore.

My heart swells and lifts just like a rising tide,
Sprightly as a lively wind that scatters the mist and
  snow,
When I think of Carra and Gallen side by side,
Schaveela's welcome and the great plains of Mayo.

At last to Killeaden, God's own garden you might say,
The finest fruit in Ireland, the pride of Mayomen,
If I were standing now among my people there,
The curse of age wither, I'd be a boy again.

(Translated from Irish by Brendan Kennelly)

J.M. SYNGE
1871-1909

From the powerful rural pageantry of his plays one might have thought John Millington Synge a west of Ireland man. In fact he was a city kid born and reared in Orwell Park, only a few hundred yards from where I grew up in Fairfield Park, Rathgar. He would have caught the same tram into college as I did, only in his time it would have been drawn by a horse. It was Synge who discovered that the speech prevalent in certain parts of Ireland was in fact semi-poetry and only had to be adapted for the theatre to provide a sort of sparkling dialogue of a kind not heard before on the stage. *The Playboy of the Western World* is one of the great plays of the twentieth century and has an affinity with another major work, Sean O'Casey's *The Plough and the Stars*, which took its dialogue from the poetry of the ordinary Dubliner's speech. Of course when both plays had their first night the Irish audience, with their genius for discerning the quality of a major work, reacted negatively and attacked the actors, as well as trying to wreck the Abbey theatre. It didn't take a feather out of Synge, however, who charitably realised that people can be confused when they first see themselves in the mirror.

The love of his life was the ravishing Molly O'Neill, who played the first Pegeen Mike in *The Playboy* and is generally held to be the greatest Abbey actress ever. But poor Synge didn't live to marry her and was buried in Glasnevin in 1909, an event anticipated in a poem he had sent to Molly a short while before.

A Question

I asked if I got sick and died, would you
With my black funeral go walking too,
If you'd stand close to hear them talk or pray
While I'm let down in that steep bank of clay.

And, No, you said, for if you saw a crew
Of living idiots, pressing round that new
Oak coffin – they alive, I dead beneath
That board, – you'd rave and rend them with your teeth.

ANONYMOUS

Irish, Welsh and Scots sport national costumes. But Ulstermen go further and add orange sashes to theirs which they treat with great reverence. There is a story about a wee Orange lad about to die and the last thing he wanted was to have a sash slipped over his tiny frame. Then, according to his mother, 'He played a wee brattle on his drum, said "To hell with the pope" and went straight into the loving arms of Jesus Christ.'

In fact, Orange marches are one of the most Irish things left to us. Despite their political theme, with their flamboyant gyrations and choreographed moves, they give an essentially Irish presentation. A Protestant clergyman who is an excellent flute player has explained to me that many of the airs to the Orange songs are re-arrangements of Irish traditional tunes. To prove this the clergyman (who is six feet three and speaks good Irish) played for me a rearranged version of a famous Orange marching song which sounded really groovy as an Irish jig. Here is the song for you.

The Sash My Father Wore

Sure I'm an Ulster Orangeman, from Erin's Isle I came
To see my Glasgow brethren all of honour and of fame,
And to tell them of my forefathers who fought in days of
    yore,
All on the twelfth day of July in the sash my father wore.

It's ould, but it's beautiful, and its colours they are fine,
It was worn at Derry, Aughrim, Enniskillen and the
    Boyne;
My father wore it in his youth in the bygone days of
    yore,
And on the Twelfth I love to wear the sash my father
    wore.

And when I'm going to leave yeeze all 'Good luck!' to
    youse I'll say,
And as I cross the raging sea my Orange flute I'll play;
Returning to my native town, to ould Belfast once more,
To be welcomed back by Orangemen in the sash my
    father wore.

ALICE MILLIGAN
1865-1953

I have often wondered why there has never been a plaque to Alice Milligan in the Abbey Theatre whose birthday is 14th September. She wrote the first of the plays *The Last of the Fianna* staged in 1900 by the Irish Literary Theatre, which inspired other poets and dramatists including Yeats to look to the tales of Fionn and Oisin for inspiration.

Alice came from a family of Unionist land owners and businessmen and, after qualifying from Methodist College Belfast and Kings College London, refused to go to Germany for postgraduate work and instead headed for Dublin where she wanted to learn Irish.

She organised for the Gaelic League all over Ireland and her patriotic poems were read around the country firesides. She also ran a socialist paper in Belfast.

Why are Ulster poets like her, Emily Lawless and Ella Young forgotten today, when their unassuming Irishness and fine verse could be a beacon for a generation who are growing up without knowing who they really are or where they come from?

from When I Was a Little Girl

When I was a little girl,
In a garden playing,
A thing was often said
To chide us delaying:

"Come in! for it's growing late,
And the grass will wet ye!
Come in! or when its dark
The Fenians will get ye."

Four little pairs of hands
In the cots where she led those,
Over their frightened heads
Pulled up the bedclothes.

But one little rebel there,
Watching all with laughter
Thought "When the Fenians come
I'll rise and go after."

Wished she had been a boy
And a good deal older –
Able to walk for miles
With a gun on her shoulder.

ROBERT BRIDGES
1844-1930

Any bit of snow reminds us of how seldom we have more than a flurry of it, compared with 1947 when there was a blizzard nearly every day from January to March. Massive snow falls were a feature of Victorian winters and the atmosphere they created is finely caught by the Poet Laureate Robert Bridges in his poem 'London Snow', where he describes how the city comes to a halt under the carpet that unfolds from the sky.

Bridges was a strange cove who wrote wodges of heavy trash, and eight worthless verse plays. Yet in between he wrote a few poems which figure in any good English poetry anthology. He did a favour to a far greater poet than himself, Gerard Manley Hopkins, when he saw to it that Hopkins's poems were published posthumously in 1918, twenty-nine years after the poet's death, although even then Bridges didn't understand most of the time what the hell his friend was talking about.

from London Snow

When men were all asleep the snow came flying,
In large white flakes falling on the city brown,
Stealthily and perpetually settling and loosely lying,
Hushing the latest traffic of the drowsy town;
Deadening, muffling, stifling its murmurs failing;
Lazily and incessantly floating down and down:
Silently sifting and veiling road, roof and railing;
Hiding difference, making unevenness even,
Into angles and crevices softly drifting and sailing.
All night it fell, and when full inches seven
It lay in the depth of its uncompacted lightness,
The clouds blew off from a high and frosty heaven;
And all woke earlier for the unaccustomed brightness
Of the winter dawning, the strange unheavenly glare:

...   .

But even for them awhile no cares encumber
Their minds diverted; the daily word is unspoken,
The daily thoughts of labour and sorrow slumber
At the sight of the beauty that greets them, for the charm
   they have broken.

SARAH CHURCHILL
1914-1982

In the 1930s a monstrous monsignor forbade the erection on Dun Laoghaire pier of one of the finest religious statues of the twentieth century. Fortunately, a few people, led by the late architect Daithi Hanley, fought for three decades against the decision and you can see today in Dun Laoghaire as you come off the pier Andrew O'Connor's spectacular monument of Christ the King with its three figures of the Redeemer, Desolation, Consolation and Triumph. It's so enormous one wonders how the monsignor could have hidden it as he did for thirty years in a solicitor's garden. I used to bring people to see the statue there lying on its side covered with leaves. Once I was lucky enough to write and act in a play in Ireland with Winston Churchill's actress daughter, and I brought her out to see the statue in the garden on Military Road, Kiliney. She was so moved by the experience that she afterwards wrote a poem about the occasion, and entitled her next book *The Unwanted Statue*. Monsignors, you know, don't always win.

from The Unwanted Statue

A three dimensioned Christ
Cast aside
In an untended back garden.

One Christ dying
Lies on its face
One Christ dead sleeps
With closed eyes
Though ligaments of one arm are torn and strained.

The third Christ lifts his body to the skies
With outstretched arms
The face bewildered, compassionate and pained.

A solicitor minds it
Custodian of the Unwanted Christ
That lies among the grasses and the weeds
And the small animals that stroke the dying face
So close to the breathing ground.

JOHN KEEGAN CASEY
1846-1870

A most underestimated Irish poet is John Keegan Casey. Luckily, Derek Warfield (of the Wolfe Tones band) also thought highly of him and devoted a lot of time in uncovering hundreds of songs and poems written by Casey who has been forgotten, perhaps due to his early death aged twenty-four after his arrest in connection with the Fenian Rising. He was well versed in traditional Irish literature, both in English and Gaelic, which enabled him to pick up themes and language to give his own work a quality which makes it outlast its time. It's hard to think of a better-written love song than 'Maire My Girl'. Robbie Burns or even Lord Byron could have been proud of this poem by a Tipperary schoolmaster.

from Maire My Girl

Over the dim blue hills
Strays a wild river,
Over the dim blue hills
Rests my heart ever,
Dearer and brighter
Than jewels and pearls,
Dwells she in beauty there,
Maire my girl.

...   .

'Twas on an April eve
That I first met her;
Many an eve shall pass
Ere I forget her.
Since my young heart has been
Wapped in a whirl,
Thinking and dreaming of
Maire my girl.

She is too kind and fond
Ever to grieve me,
She has too pure a heart
E'er to deceive me.
Were I Tyrconnell's chief
Or Desmond's earl,
Life would be dark, wanting
Maire my girl.

...   .

THE HON. EMILY LAWLESS
1845-1913

These days when thousands pour into the country each month we might remind ourselves of a time when it was the other way round. After the Battle of the Boyne in 1690 there was a mass exodus of Irishmen to the continent; it was calculated that by the middle of the eighteenth century over four hundred thousand Irishmen serving in the armies of France, Germany, Austria, Russia and Spain (as described on page 25, 'The Battle Eve of the Brigade' by Thomas Davis). These became known as the Wild Geese. No one has written better about them (even our dear Thomas Davis) than the novelist daughter of Lord Cloncurry, the Honourable Emily Lawless, whose summer residence was Maretimo House with its bridge which you can see from the Dart as you travel between Blackrock and Seapoint. She was one of the best-known novelists and poets of her time and much admired by Gladstone for her novel *Hurrish* about the Irish Land War. Perhaps her finest book is *The Wild Geese*, a collection of poems devoted to those gallant eighteenth-century Irish gentlemen who had to leave their own country when they 'were worsted in the game' by King Billy after the Battle of Aughrim.

76

from Clare Coast (c. 1720)

Mockers, bemocked by time.
War-dogs, hungry and grey,
Gnawing a naked bone,
Fighters in every clime,
Every cause but our own.

Fool, did you never hear
Of sunshine which broke through rain?
Sunshine which came with storm?
Laughter that rang of pain?
Boastings begotten of grief,
Vauntings to hide a smart,
Braggings with trembling lip,
Tricks of a broken heart?

See, beneath us our boat
Tugs at its tightening chain,
Holds out its sail to the breeze,
Pants to be gone again.
Off then with shouts and mirth,
Off with laughter and jests,
Jests and song on our lips,
Hearts like lead in our breasts.

ANONYMOUS

Northern Protestants have a specific sense of humour, which they share with Northern Catholics, and which is not always understood as it might be by the English. Take the famous song for instance 'The Old Orange Flute'. It has a flavour that can only be found on this last island on the edge of Europe. It tells the tale of a Protestant flute player who married a Catholic and went to live in 'Connaught' where he attempted to play his flute in the Catholic Church choir. But the stubborn wee thing just wouldn't play papist hymns. All they could get out of it was 'Kick the Pope' and the 'Boyne Water'. In the end the flute had to be burned alive, but as it went up in flames it defiantly piped out anti-papist barbs. Actually, some English folk might find the ballad a little in bad taste, but both sides of the community here sing it with great relish. That's Ireland.

from The Old Orange Flute

In the County Tyrone, in the town of Dungannon,
Where many a ruction myself had a han' in,
Bob Williamson lived, a weaver by trade
And all of us thought him a stout Orange blade.
On the Twelfth of July as around it would come,
Bob played on the flute to the sound of the drum.
You may talk of your harp, your piano or lute
But there's nothing compared with the ould Orange
    flute.

Till after some time at the priest's desire
He went with his old flute to play in the choir.
He went with his old flute to play for the Mass
And the instrument shivered and sighed: 'Oh, alas!'
And blow as he would, though it made a great noise,
The flute would play only 'The Protestant Boys.'

At a council of priests that was held the next day,
They decided to banish the old flute away
For they couldn't knock heresy out of its head
And they bought Bob a new one to play in its stead.
So the old flute was doomed and its fate was pathetic,
'Twas fastened and burned at the stake as heretic,
While the flames roared around it they heard a strange
    noise –
'Twas the old flute still whistling 'The Protestant Boys'.

(Nineteenth century)

RUPERT BROOKE
1887-1915

When we marvel at the way many were prepared to risk their lives in the Easter Rising of 1916 it's easy to forget that giving your life for your country was regarded then in a different light than it is today. When the Great War broke out in 1914 the English upper class poured out of the public schools and Oxford and Cambridge to join up under the Union Jack. In fact, English society never really recovered from the loss of 70 per cent of young men of the leader class who were wiped out in the trenches during the Great War. The most famous of them was Rupert Brooke, a golden lad with film star looks who fortunately was also a gifted poet and left behind a heritage of verse before dying at Gallipoli in 1915. There is in his sonnet 'The Dead' something of the same spirit that Patrick Pearse and James Connolly inculcated in their followers when they made their stand in the Post Office ninety-one years ago.

The Dead

Blow out, you bugles, over the rich Dead!
There's none of these so lonely and poor of old,
But, dying, has made us rarer gifts than gold.
These laid the world away; poured out the red
Sweet wine of youth; gave up the years to be
Of work and joy, and that unhoped serene,
That men call age; and those who would have been,
Their sons, they gave, their immortality.

Blow, bugles, blow! They brought us, for our dearth,
Holiness, lacked so long, and Love, and Pain.
Honour has come back, as a king, to earth,
And paid his subjects with a royal wage;
And Nobleness walks in our ways again;
And we have come into our heritage.

BRENDAN BEHAN
1923-1964

The poem below might have been written by an eighth century Irish monk in his cell at the edge of Glendalough Lake. It was written in a cell all right (in Gaelic), but in Mountjoy prison and the poet was Brendan Behan. Brendan always wrote his poems in Irish because he felt he could craft words better in his native tongue. In this translation from the original you can see the marvellous run of words beginning with the same letter which was a feature of early Gaelic poetry, and which Brendan had the knack of. Surprisingly enough, a number of his poems had religious themes. Sister Monica, the head of William Street School, had taught him his prayers when he was six and told his mother that 'she was rearing a genius'. In his last hours in the Meath Hospital when a visiting nun mopped his fevered brow with a cold compress, he murmured 'God bless you sister. May you be the mother of a bishop.'

The Coming of Spring

Wild wicked winter
Your harsh face I hate.
The North wind blows in
Trembling, tormented, tough,
Without growth or goodness,
Loveliness or love,
Till the white feast of Brigid
And the resurrection of joy.

Then comes the South wind,
Promise of heat for my limbs
Life leaping in me,
Awakening of the blood.
Winter, you wastrel,
Old age is your season.
Welcome and a thousand more to you,
O Spring of my youth.

(Translated from the Irish by Ulick O'Connor)

JOSEPH PLUNKETT
1887-1916

A major achievement of the Taoiseach's is that he has made the 1916 Rising respectable once more. Now with the Northern situation well advanced we are for the first time in a position to have a detached look at what happened in Easter week. Looking at the names of the signatories on the proclamation, what is remarkable is the sheer achievement of every one of them. Thomas MacDonagh was a brilliant university lecturer; Pearse a hugely innovative school headmaster; James Connolly had the enviable gift of being able to express in crystal clear prose ideas that marked him as one of the advanced social thinkers of the twentieth century; Joseph Plunkett made the first colour photograph in Ireland, constructed a much admired strategic military plan for the Rising, and built a wireless transmitter to broadcast news of the Rising in the United States, as well as writing 'I See His Blood Upon the Rose', a famous poem which is known throughout the world to many people including her Imperial Highness Princess Michiko of Japan.

With real style he married, in his cell, a beautiful Dublin girl, Grace Gifford, a few hours before he was executed. Here is another poem of his to show that 'I See His Blood' wasn't just a one off.

The Stars Sang in God's Garden

The stars sang in God's garden,
The stars are the birds of God;
The night-time is God's harvest,
It's fruits are the words of God.

God ploughed his fields in the morning,
God sowed his seed at noon,
God reaped and gathered in his corn
With the rising of the moon.

The sun rose up at midnight,
The sun rose red as blood,
It showed the Reaper, the dead Christ,
Upon his cross of wood.

For many live that one may die,
And one must die that many live –
The stars are silent in the sky
Lest my poor songs be fugitive.

GEORGE KENNEDY ALLEN BELL
1883-1958

George Kennedy Allen Bell, Bishop of Chichester, was a splendid man. In 1942, when the Second World War was at it's height, he condemned his own country's terror bombing of civilians in the German cities. This may have prevented him from becoming Archbishop of Canterbury, but has left him in history as a hero of his time.

Bishop Bell was a fine poet and had lent his cathedral at Chichester for the first presentation of T.S. Elliot's play *Murder in the Cathedral*. At Oxford, Bell had won the Newdigate poetry prize and was a close friend of a fellow student, Dubliner Oliver St. John Gogarty. The two of them exchanged letters which when collected run to over hundreds of thousands of words. I am pleased to say I was responsible for saving these letters from destruction by his executors after his death (they had been placed with me by his wife). Bishop Bell, whose favourite saint was Francis of Assisi, never complained about the treatment he received from the establishment simply because he had had the courage to tell the truth.

from Nobody's Friend

Then NOBODIES of a different sort
I tried to help, as a Christian ought,
When Hitler sent across the seas
Thousands of pitiful refugees.
NOBODY more completely hated
The Nazi system – vile – ill-fated!
But NOBODY loved me when I found
A better Germany underground.
There were other moments, during the war,
When people thought I went too far;
Pleading against the obliteration
Either of city or of nation.
But I will not trouble you more tonight
With further evidence of my plight.
I hope you'll agree, now I come to an end,
I can justly claim to be NOBODY'S FRIEND.

HILAIRE BELLOC
1870-1953

It's because it breathes magic that real poetry is so rare. It can bring a scene up before the mind so that you can almost see and smell it. People who have never been to Sligo can scent it from a Yeats poem. Shropshire is perhaps the best-known county in England by people who have never been there, because of Housman's verse. The great poet of Southern England, Hilaire Belloc, who drank his way through a lifetime of fine wines, interspersed with sailing and walking on the Sussex hills, left a testament of hymns to his home county which can still stir the mind.

Sadly, the England Belloc loved was out of fashion when he died. A poem like the one below, however, is always in fashion as landscape doesn't change.

from The South Country

When I am living in the Midlands,
That are sodden and unkind,
I light my lamp in the evening:
My work is left behind;
And the great hills of the South Country
Come back into my mind.

The great hills of the South Country
They stand along the sea,
And it's there, walking in the high woods,
That I could wish to be,
And the men that were boys when I was a boy
Walking along with me.

But the men that live in the South Country
Are the kindest and most wise,
They get their laughter from the loud surf,
And the faith in their happy eyes
Comes surely from our Sister the Spring
When over the sea she flies;
The violets suddenly bloom at her feet,
She blesses us with surprise.

I will gather and carefully make my friends
Of the men of the Sussex Weald,
They watch the stars from silent folds,
they stiffly plough the field.
By them and the God of the south Country
My poor soul shall be healed.

CHRISTOPHER MARLOWE
1564-1593

The Elizabethan age was a glorious one in English literature. Words flew like butterflies from the lips of poets and playwrights as the English language was forged into the beautiful instrument of speech it would become. This was the age of Shakespeare, Marlowe, Ben Jonson, and Fletcher. The youngest of the set was Christopher Marlowe who used to meet with the others in the Mermaid Tavern after rehearsals in the Globe theatre. It was Marlowe who created the cult of the 'mighty line' with which the great playwrights of the time could bring an audience shouting to their feet. He was also a bit of a lad, inclined to the odd fight during one of which he was knifed to death at the age of twenty-two. The dramatic passage that made him famous, as an aria in an opera might establish the name of a librettist, appears in his play *The Tragic History of Dr. Faustus* which tells of a man who has sold his soul to the devil in return for a promise to bring back from history whatever character he might most desire. Faustus chooses Helen of Troy.

From Dr. Faustus

Was this the face that launch'd a thousand ships,
And burnt the topless towers of Ilium?
Sweet Helen, make me immortal with a kiss. –
Her lips suck forth my soul: see, where it flies! –
Come, Helen, come, give me my soul again.
Here will I dwell, for heaven is in these lips,
And all is dross that is not Helena.
I will combat with weak Menelaus,
And wear thy colours on my plumed crest;
Yes I will wound Achilles in the heel
And then return to Helen for a kiss
O, thou art fairer than the evening air
Clad in the beauty of a thousand stars;
More lovely than the monarch of the sky
In wanton Arethusa's azur'd arms;
And none but thou shalt be my paramour!

KATHERINE TYNAN
1861-1931

These days, if a woman writer deigns to write about her father, he is often portrayed as a mixture of Judas Iscariot and Dracula. But the fine Irish poetess Katherine Tynan adored her parent and kept his memory alive in her writing. He was a rich farmer who owned land at Newlands Cross, Dublin and kept an open house for the poets of the 1890s, such as W.B. Yeats, George Russell and women poets like Eithne Carbery and Ella Young.

Katherine became a big hit in London at the turn of the century and was accepted in a literary set that included Oscar Wilde, the Rossettis and Alice Meynell. But she never forgot those happy days at the foot of the Dublin hills where, under the loving guidance of her father, she had become a poetess. Her other hero was Parnell and she is one of those who, at his funeral, saw 'the most glorious meteor sail across the clear space of the heaven and fall suddenly.'

The poem here to her father catches the atmosphere of the landscape of the beautiful pasture lands under the mountain that hang above Tallaght and Clondalkin. The estate today has been acquired by the Irish Rugby Football Union.

Alas, the Tynan house, which in another country would be a national monument, has fallen on bad times: yet another black mark against what laughably passes in Dublin for a city council.

To the Beloved

You were part of the green country,
Of the grey hills and the quiet places;
They are not the same, the fields and the mountains,
Without the lost and beloved faces,
And you were a part of the sweet country.

There's a road that winds by the foot of the mountains
Where I run in my dreams and you come to meet me,
With your blue eyes and your cheeks' old roses,
The old fond smile that was quick to greet me.
They are not the same, the fields and the mountains.

You were part of the fields and mountains,
Everyone knew you, everyone loved you;
All the world was your friend and neighbour,
The women smiled and the men approved you,
They are not the same, the fields and the mountains.

I sigh no more for the pleasant places,
The longer I've lost you the more I miss you.
My heart seeks you in dreams and shadows,
In dreams I find you, in dreams I kiss you,
And wake, alas! To the lovely places.

ROBIN FLOWER
1881-1946

If you played rugby or soccer three decades or so ago you were regarded as a traitor to Ireland by the GAA. I did play these games but was lucky enough not to have been turned against Gaelic culture by that silly ban. I came in contact with an elite breed of Gaelic scholars (Norwegian, Swedish, German as well as Irish) who really had a handle on the true Gaelic Ireland. They had come over here and discovered a culture in Ireland equal to that of the Egyptians and the Greeks, and a living civilisation on the lips of the native speakers in places like the Blaskets and the Aran islands. Their scholars' eyes would kindle with delight as they recited to you some recent find as if they had unseamed a ridge of gold. One of them, a Yorkshire man, Robin Flower, was known on the Blaskets as *'Blaithin'* (the flower). Though this translation of his is short, the last line comes in with the force of a steam engine coming round a corner.

At Mass

AH! Light, lovely lady with delicate lips aglow!
With breast more white than a branch heavy-laden with
    snow!
When my hand was lifted at Mass to salute the Host
I looked at you once and the half of my soul was lost.

CHARLES BAUDELAIRE
1821-1867

Want to get away? Feel the caress of the sun and the soothing embrace of the blue waters? Walk along the golden pathway of a beach? This is the sort of guff we read in the windows of the travel agents today. How much more agreeable if an astute travel agent would use Baudelaire's splendid poem 'The Wine of Lovers' as an advertising brochure for a sunny holiday rather than the fake language of the hired copywriter.

The Wine of Lovers

What a space we have today;
No bridle, bit, or spur to stay
Our rapture; as we roam the sky
Wine as our horse, you and I.

Like two reckless angels driven
By a fevered sea towards heaven,
In the crystal blue of morning
Follow the mirage that's forming.

Balanced gently on the wings
Of friendly whirlwinds let us glide,
Share the delirium that it brings.

My sister, swimming side by side,
We'll skim the surface till it seems
We've reached the Eden of my dreams.

(Translated by Ulick O'Connor)

DONAGH MACDONAGH
1912-1968

University College Dublin in the early 1930s hit an intellectual peak. A brilliant group reigned there at the time which included Myles na gCopaleen, Denis Devlin, Cearbhall O'Dalaigh (later Chief Justice), Charlie Donnelly (who wrote *Even the Olives are Bleeding*) and Cyril Cusack. Donagh Mac-Donagh was a small little man with a slight hunch who wrote one of the best verse plays in English since Yeats's time – *Happy as Larry*. He was very much a Dubliner. One remembers him in Groome's Hotel after hours where he could assail you with a forked tongue if he didn't like what you had written about his plays.

I don't think anyone has caught the tension between Dubliner and culchie better than MacDonagh, who as a district justice in the country had to listen to many a rural tale while sitting on the bench.

from Dublin Made Me

Dublin made me and no little town
With the country closing in on its streets
The cattle walking proudly on its pavements
The jobbers, the gombeenmen and the cheats

Devouring the fair-day between them
A public-house to half a hundred men
And the teacher, the solicitor and the bank-clerk
In the hotel bar drinking for ten

Dublin made me, not the secret poteen still
The raw and hungry hills on the West
The lean road flung over profitless bog
Where only a snipe could nest.

I disclaim all fertile meadows, all tilled land
The evil that grows from it and the good,
But the Dublin of old statutes, the arrogant city,
Stirs proudly and secretly in my blood.

E.E. CUMMINGS
1894-1962

As you read this poem you might think a sub-editor has goofed just because there are no capital letters or title there. But the American poet E.E. Cummings didn't believe in punctuation, higher case or titles. He just loved to tumble words like a juggler and he felt that capital letters could get in the way of slick presentation. Cummings was considered the cat's pyjamas in the 1920s, perhaps too much so which is why he's largely forgotten today, while genial fakes who were his contemporaries and whose only talent was to hide the fact that they had none are still pushed in front of your puss. His rhymes are hilarious. No one yet has found an adequate rhyme for statues but Cummings came up with this :

> 'gimme the he-man's solid bliss
> for youse ideas i'll match youse
> a pretty girl who naked is
> is worth a million statues'

Here is a sonnet about the age old problem of what's a man to do when he finds his favourite bird has left him.

it may not always be so;and i say
that if your lips,which i have loved,should touch
another's,and your dear strong fingers clutch
his heart,as mine in time not far away;
if on another's face your sweet hair lay
in such a silence as i know,or such
great writhing words as,uttering overmuch.
stand helplessly before the spirit at bay;

if this should be,i say if this should be –
you of my heart,send me a little word;
that i may go unto him,and take his hands,
saying,Accept all happiness from me.
then shall i turn my face,and hear one bird
sing terribly afar in the lost lands.

FORREST REID
1875-1947

Forrest Reid. No it's not a film actor's name you should know about. Forrest Reid was an Irish novelist from Belfast who seems to have been absolutely forgotten. Yet he was a good enough writer for E.M. Forster, the best English novelist of his time, to look for permission to dedicate one of his novels to. Cute old Henry James was also an admirer of Reid's prose, but nearly had a fit when Reid's second novel, *The Garden of God* (1905), the story of a love affair between two young men, was dedicated to him. Reid was the son of a Belfast mercantile ship owner and spent most of his life there which he wrote about beautifully in *Apostate*, a sort of Belfast equivalent of Joyce's *A Portrait of an Artist as a Young Man*. I hadn't known about Forrest Reid as a poet until I discovered this one by him, about autumn in his native city, which Lennox Robinson included in his marvellous *Golden Treasury of Irish Verse*.

from Autumn

Slowly, one by one,
Through the damp-smelling, misty air of autumn
  the delicate leaves drop down,
Covering the grass like a carpet-
A carpet woven in gold and silver:--
And the sun,
Shining through the bare black trees,
Turns to a glory of gold these dying woods.

Let the winds scatter
The broken scarlet web of autumn wide over the world!
Soft with sleep,
Let the delicate air sigh through the naked branches,
That still preserve their beauty.

Gone, gone, is their merriment. Only an echo remains
  while the curtain of night is descending;
But how lovely that echo! --
Lovelier far than the shouts and the laughter, the
  songs and the childish play: --
Lovely as autumn.

WILLIAM WORDSWORTH
1770-1850

Will there be snow or not this year? Up to a few decades ago the question didn't arise. We knew we would be snow-bound for a week or so in winter before the April buds came out. One remembers in 1947 the dog pond in the Phoenix Park frozen for a month and packed with skaters so that if the ice had cracked a sizeable section of the population would have snuffed it. It snowed that year every day for six weeks starting in January. Two decades later, after another ferocious winter, there was still snow on the Feather Bed Mountain in May. It may seem somewhat unreal now. But perhaps we can bring before the mind's eye a memory of what it was like from a description by William Wordsworth of an outing before global warming set in. So let's skate.

from The Prelude

All shod with steel,
We hiss'd along the polish'd ice, in games
Confederate, imitative of the chase
And woodland pleasures, the resounding horn,
The Pack loud bellowing, and the hunted hare.
So through the darkness and the cold we flew,
And not a voice was idle; with the din,
Meanwhile, the precipices rang aloud,
The leafless trees, and every icy crag
Tinkled like iron, while the distant hills
Into the tumult sent an alien sound
Of melancholy, not unnoticed, while the stars,
Eastward, were sparkling clear, and in the west
The orange sky of evening died away.

Eva Gore-Booth
1870-1926

In an extraordinary talk on RTÉ radio Ruth Dudley Edwards referred to Countess Constance Markievicz as a 'self-indulgent, blood-thirsty murderer, a fraud and an exhibitionist.' It is Edwards herself who with her name-calling is self-indulgent. None of these allegations were remotely true. Yeats, a better judge, in a memorable phrase referred to Constance and her sister Eva Gore-Booth as 'two girls in silk kimonos, both beautiful, one a gazelle'.

Eva was a pacifist who led the campaign to stop Roger Casement's execution. She became an important figure in the Socialist Party in Manchester where among her other achievements she formed a trade union for women circus acrobats. Her poetry is still underestimated though the one below, 'The Little Waves of Breffny', can still be found in many anthologies. At college we used to affectionately call Ruth Dudley Edwards' father, who was a brilliant history professor, 'Deadly Bad Words'. It might be an apt title for Madame Ruth in the present context, not meaning it in this case as a joke.

from The Little Waves of Breffny

The grand road from the mountain goes shining to the
   sea,
And there is traffic in it, and many a horse and cart,
But the little roads of Cloonagh are dearer far to me,
And the little roads of Cloonagh go rambling through
   my heart.

A great storm from the ocean goes shouting o'er the hill,
And there is glory in it and terror on the wind,
But the haunted air of twilight is very strange and still,
And the little winds of twilight are dearer to my mind.

The great waves of the Atlantic sweep storming on their
   way,
Shining green and silver with the hidden herring shoal,
But the Little Waves of Breffny have drenched my heart
   in spray
But the Little Waves of Breffny go stumbling through my
   soul.

SIEGFRIED SASSOON
1886-1967

Siegfried Sassoon came from landed English gentry but was unsympathetic to the military ethic of his class. As a captain in the First World War, when he had won the Military Cross for gallantry, he proceeded to mount a fierce campaign against what he regarded as the wickedness of the war his country was fighting. He was the first of the poets to do so and, along with his protégé Wilfred Owen, helped to turn the tide of opinion towards the carnage that was taking place in France. Sassoon had a powerful influence on his time, both as pacifist and poet. He was a modest man who charmingly underestimated his own gifts, summing up his success as a poet as follows: 'I chanced on the device of composing two or three harsh peremptory and colloquial stanzas with a knockout blow in the last line.'

They

The Bishop tells us: 'When the boys come back
They will not be the same; for they'll have fought
In a just cause: they lead the last attack
On Anti-Christ; their comrades' blood has bought
New right to breed an honourable race,
They have challenged Death and dared him face to face.'

'We're none of us the same!' the boys reply.
'For George lost both his legs; and Bill's stone blind;
Poor Jim's shot through the lungs and like to die;
And Bert's gone syphilitic: you'll not find
A chap who's served that hasn't found some change!'
And the Bishop said: 'The ways of God are strange!'

WILLIAM BEDELL STANFORD
1910-1991

A problem when the new Irish state came into being in 1922 was how to reconcile the new ruling class with those they displaced. The vast majority of the Anglo-Irish Protestant community had been in the saddle for hundreds of years. Now it was their turn to be on the ground looking up at someone else in their place. To their credit, from the very start a number of leading merchants and landlords accepted nomination to the Seanad and made an invaluable contribution over the first ten years to the progress of the Irish Free State. In the late 1940s William Bedell Stanford, Regius Professor of Greek at Trinity College, was elected to the Seanad. For the next nineteen years he was to make a massive contribution, reaffirming in the tradition of Grattan and Tone what it meant to be truly Irish. Bedell Stanford was one of the most handsome men in Dublin and visitors used to gaze at him in awe as he strode across the cobblestones in Trinity with his professor's robes streaming in the wind. Besides being one of the great Greek scholars of his day, Bedell was also a poet and the following poem by him from the *Penguin Book of Irish Verse* refers in the second last line to the instinctive fear in the Irish mind of the Formorians, 'the men from under the sea'.

Undertone

When the landfolk of Galway converse with a stranger,
softly the men speak, more softly the women,
light words on their lips, and an accent that sings
in traditional cadences (once plucked by harpists
to cheer melancholic carousals of kings),
when the landfolk of Galway converse with a stranger.

But under the cadences, under the light lips,
under the lilt of the harp-plucking bard,
threaded deep in its socket of anger and loneliness
a passion, with piercing and tightening screw, grips
their minds' inner engine and presses it hard.

When the landfolk of Galway converse with a stranger,
softly the men speak, more softly the women;
yet older than harp-playing, older than welcomes,
and undertone threatens Formorian danger,
when the landfolk of Galway converse with a stranger.

RUPERT BROOKE
1887-1915

In late summer, when the seasons begin to blend, the skies on these islands fill with the most wonderful rolling clouds. Bernard Shaw used maintain that the Irish skies were the most beautiful in the world, but the best tribute to our mutual Atlantic skyscapes has been written by the soldier-poet Rupert Brooke in his poem 'Clouds'. He sees the great caravansary of clouds which move across the sky as a representation of the souls of men and women released from their earthly prison in the grave. Brooke's literary heroes included the Irish poets James Stephen's and W.B. Yeats, and he was much impressed one day when Yeats asked him where he got his shirts made. The old boy wanted to pick one that would spruce himself up in the mornings. In his most famous poem, 'The Soldier', written before his death at Gallipoli, Brooke expressed the wish that his poems might 'give somewhere back the thoughts by England given'. In 'Clouds' he has done just that.

Clouds

Down the blue night the unending columns press
In the noiseless tumult, break and wave and flow,
Now tread the far South, or lift rounds of snow
Up to the white moon's hidden loveliness.

Some pause in their grave wandering comradeless,
And turn with profound gesture vague and slow,
As who would pray good for the world, but know
Their benediction empty as they bless.

They say that the Dead die not, but remain
Near to the rich heirs of their grief and mirth.
I think they ride the calm mid-heaven, as these,
In wise majestic melancholy train,
And watch the moon, and the still-raging seas,
And men, coming and going on the earth.

WILLIAM SHAKESPEARE
1564-1616

The late Leo Rowsome, prince of the uileann pipes, used to be able to play the air of the` Red Fox' (`An Maidrín Rua') in such a way that you could hear the sounds of the hunt coming through the music. It was an extraordinary feat which reminded me of a passage in *A Midsummer Night's Dream* where two characters reminisce about their hunting days in language which Shakespeare wrote to echo the yelping and barking of the hounds pushing their way through the grass with their masters urging them on behind. Reading out loud this piece of dialogue from the play, between Queen Hippolyta and the Duke of Athens, can wing the mind back to the Cretan hunting fields of old with the hounds in full cry.

from A Midsummer Night's Dream

Hippolyta: I was with Hercules and Cadmus once,
When in a wood of Crete they bay'd the bear
With hounds of Sparta: never did I hear
Such gallant chiding; such sweet thunder

Theseus   My hounds are bred out of the Spartan kind,
So flew'd, so sanded; and their heads are hung
With ears that sweep away the morning dew;
Crook-knee'd and dew-lapp'd like Thessalian
  bulls;
Slow in pursuit, but match'd in mouth like
  bells;
Each under each. A cry more tuneable
Was never holla'd to, nor cheer'd with horn,
In Crete, in Sparta, nor in Thessaly:

PATRICK MACDONOGH
1902-1961

No Irish poet is more underestimated than Patrick Mac-
Donogh. He began his writing life publishing quite ordinary
verse. Then half way through his career he suddenly went
into top gear and produced a series of magnificent poems
culminating in his last book, *One Landscape Still*. A striking
factor of his art is his ability to unleash an enthralling first line
whose melody he plays on throughout the poem. Take this for
example: 'O she walked unaware of her own increasing
beauty.'

If the poet can keep that up he's on his bicycle. And Mac-
Donogh does in the extraordinary poem below. The searing
sadness of the last verse was echoed by MacDonogh's own life
for he died tragically by his own hand in 1961. In his early
years Patrick and his brother W.P. were probably the two best
hockey half-backs in the world, playing on the wonderful
Irish side that were number one in Europe from 1936 to 1939.

from She Walked Unaware

Oh, she walked unaware of her own increasing beauty
That was holding men's thoughts from market or
    plough,
As she passed by intent on her womanly duties
And she without leisure to be wayward or proud;
Or if she had pride then it was not in her thinking
But thoughtless in her body like a flower of good
    breeding.
The first time I saw her spreading coloured linen
Beyond the green willow she gave me gentle greeting
With no more intention than the leaning willow tree.

……   …..   …..   …..   …..   …..   …..

October is spreading bright flame along stripped
    willows,
Low fires of the dogwood burn down to grey water –
God pity me now and all desolate sinners
Demented with beauty! I have blackened my thought
In drouths of bad longing, and all brightness goes
    shrouded
Since he came with his rapture of wild words that
    mirrored
Her beauty and made her ungentle and proud.
Tonight she will spread her brown hair on his pillow,
But I shall be hearing the harsh cries of wild fowl.

WALTER SAVAGE LANDOR
1775-1864

Yeats thought the English poet Walter Savage Landor as great
as Keats or Rossetti. Landor lived to be eighty-nine so his life
is neatly divided between two eras. The extraordinary thing is
that at a time when many English people thought of us only in
terms of peasants who kept pigs in their houses, Landor
should have been so aware of the ancient pre-Christian cul-
ture of the Gael.

His poem commemorating Tara is the best answer I know
to the bureaucrats and developers who propose to drive a
road through a shrine which is as important in archaeological
terms to Western culture as the pyramids are to the Middle
East.

from Last Fruit Off an Old Tree

Ireland never was contented …
Say you so? you are demented.
Ireland was contented when
All could use the sword and pen,
And when Tara rose so high
That her turrets split the sky,
And about her courts were seen
Liveried Angels robed in green,
Wearing, by Saint Patrick's bounty,
Emeralds big as half a county.

JAMES CLARENCE MANGAN
1803-1849

It is strange how two poets could write in almost the same way about a subject without having met one another. James Clarence Mangan, when he wrote 'And Then No More' in the 1840s, could not have known that twenty years later the greatest poet of the century, Baudelaire, would have written 'A Une Passante', an almost identical poem in French.

Both wrote about a beautiful girl they had seen for a few seconds passing by on the street, and knew at that instance they were in love with her and she with them. But neither ever saw the girl again. Baudelaire asks at the end of his poem 'The Passerby':

> 'A flash of lightning – night – beauty fled
> In whose glance I have been suddenly reborn
> Shall I see you in another world instead?'

Like Baudelaire, Mangan was leading a wretched existence as little more than a book boy in Trinity College Library, scampering like an owl up among the bookshelves, earning a pittance and ending his nights paralytic in the Fishamble Street pubs nearby. But from their sorrows both poets got poetry and probably that gave them a little happiness.

from And Then No More

I saw her once, one little while, and then no more:
'Twas Eden's light on Earth awhile, and then no more.
Amid the throng she passed along the meadow-floor:
Spring seemed to smile on Earth awhile, and then no
　　more:
But whence she came, which way she went, what garb
　　she wore
I noted not; I gazed awhile, and then no more!

I saw her once, one little while, and then no more:
Earth looked like Heaven a little while, and then no
　　more.
Her presence thrilled and lighted to its inner core
My desert breast a little while, and then no more.
So may, perchance, a meteor glance at midnight o'er
Some ruined pile a little while, and then no more!

…　　　…　　　…　　　…　　　…　　　…

121

DÁIBHÍ Ó BRUADAIR
1625-1698

Before the English were in the saddle here there were schools
where you could train to be a poet just like going to a modern
sports academy to improve your performance. Classical
Gaelic poetry was encouraged by the Irish chieftains whose
culture was drenched with poetry and music. Dáibhí Ó
Bruadair of Limerick, who died in 1698, was the last product
of these Bardic schools. With the fall of the Gaelic gentry, po-
ets like Ó Bruadair became wandering bards and their work
with all its jewelled beauty was recited in pubs and at the fire-
side.

One of his most popular poems was a savage attack writ-
ten in verse about a barmaid who had insulted him one day in
a Limerick pub. Ó Bruadair had asked for a drink and the
woman replied, 'Have you any money?' The poet said he
wasn't asking for money but only asking for drink, where-
upon the husky lassie grabbed him by the neck and threw him
out on the street. Ó Bruadair kept his powder dry, however,
and put her into a poem, a devastating revenge at a time when
poetry had the place in public life like pop music has today.
Three hundred years later Ó Bruadair's reply was brilliantly
translated by the leprechaun-like James Stephens (1880-1950),
whom I suspect may have had a similar experience in a public
house where his acerbic tongue kept the bartenders on their
toes.

A Glass of Beer

The lanky hank of a she in the pub over there
Nearly killed me for asking the loan of a glass of beer;
May the devil grip the whey-faced slut by the hair,
And beat bad manners out of her skin for a year.

That half boiled ape, with the toughest jaw you will see
On virtue's path, and voice that would rasp the dead,
Came roaring and raging the minute she looked at me,
And threw me out of the house on the back of my head!

If I asked her master he'd give me a barrel a day;
But she, with the beer at hand, not a drop would arrange!
May she marry a ghost and bear him a kitten, and may
The High King of Glory permit her to get the mange.

JAMES STEPHENS
1883-1950

Twenty years ago, from where I live in Rathgar, I could be in the Dublin mountains at Kilakee among the heather in twenty minutes, or on an enchanting beach at Sandymount in much about the same time. This is one of the reasons Bernard Shaw called Dublin the most beautiful city in Europe, even superior to Naples with its famous bay. But it's going, my friends, it's going. Great bulldozers are crashing through the undergrowth in the hills, and at the centre of the bay in Dun Laoghaire the Council have vandalised the magical seafront by building horrible high-rise buildings which hang like artificial stage drops masking Sir Thomas Deane's incomparable Town Hall.

At the time when the poet James Stephens wrote this poem about goats in the Dublin hills he could get the tram to Terenure and only canter a mile or two to where, something of a little goat himself, he could communicate with his fellow creatures.

from **The Goat Paths**

The crooked paths go every way
Upon the hill – they wind about
Through the heather in and out
Of the quiet sunniness.
And there the goats, day after day,
Stray in the sunny quietness,
Cropping here and cropping there,
As they pause and turn and pass,
Now a bit of heather spray,
Now a mouthful of the grass.

If you approach they run away,
They leap and stare, away they bound
With a sudden angry sound,
To the sunny quietude;
Crouching down where nothing stirs
In the silence of the furze,
Crouching down again to brood
In the sunny solitude.

In that airy quietness
I would think as long as they;
Through the quiet sunniness
I would stray away to brook
By a hidden beaten way
In a sunny solitude.
I would think until I found
Something I can never find,
Something lying on the ground,
In the bottom of my mind.

Æ
George Russell
1867-1935

The one hundred and fortieth anniversary of the birth of George Russell, poet and patriot, has passed without a murmur. Through ferocious work and self-sacrifice George Russell (known as Æ) laid the foundations for the Cooperative Movement which freed Irish small farmers from the greed of the gombeen man. He founded and edited *The Irish Statesman,* a superb weekly journal which cleared the fug out of many post-revolutionary minds. President Roosevelt used him as an advisor on his revolutionary New Deal and Henry Wallace, Roosevelt's Secretary of State, was much influenced by the social innovations of the poet from Rathgar.

One should not forget also Æ's stature as a painter. I have seen a George Russell portrait of Lady Gregory beside a John Butler Yeats and a Manet and it is not out of place. Æ, the gentlest of men, had his dark moments too. In this poem, after a period of despair, he tells how he regained his faith in the human spirit through the laughter of children and the glow of the grass.

Reconciliation

I begin through the grass once again to be bound to the
    Lord;
I can see, through a face that has faded, the face full of
    rest
Of the earth, of the mother, my heart with her heart in
    accord,
As I lie 'mid the cool green tresses that mantle her breast
I begin with the grass once again to be bound to the
    Lord.

By the hand of a child I am led to the throne of the King,
For a touch that now fevers me not is forgotten and far,
And His infinite sceptred hands that sway us can bring
Me in dreams from the laugh of a child to the song of a
    star.
On the laugh of a child I am borne to the joy of the King.

WILLIAM WORDSWORTH
1770-1850

Daffodils inspire many poets. Our old friend Bill Shakespeare is as usual at the head of the posse. In *A Winter's Tale* he depicts the daffodil as a pretty girl arriving first to get ahead of the party.

> '[…] Daffodils,
> That come before the swallow dares, and take
> The winds of March with beauty;'

A really fine poem in the daff genre is by William Wordsworth who, out for a walk by Lake Windermere with his sister Dorothy, got the inspiration for a piece that was to become the most popular of all his poems. The wind was blowing and the daffodils had run riot among the mossy stones when his sister noted how 'some of the daffodils rested their heads upon the stones as on a pillow for weariness and the rest tossed and reeled and danced and seemed as if they laughed'. After he had written the poem, Wordsworth was decent enough to attribute the lines 'They flash upon the inward eye / Which is the bliss of solitude;' to his sister and assert they were the best in the poem. What do you think?

from I Wandered Lonely as a Cloud

I wandered lonely as a cloud
That floats on high o'er vales and hills,
When all at once I saw a crowd,
A host, of golden daffodils;
Beside the lake, beneath the trees,
fluttering and dancing in the breeze.

Continuous as the stars that shine
And twinkle on the milky way,
They stretched in never-ending line
Along the margin of a bay:
Ten thousand saw I at a glance,
Tossing their heads in sprightly dance.

...   .

For oft, when on my couch I lie
In vacant or in pensive mood,
They flash upon the inward eye
Which is the bliss of solitude;
And then my heart with pleasure fills
And dances with the daffodils.
The waves beside them danced; but they
Out-did the sparkling waves in glee:
A poet could not but be gay,
In such a jocund company:
I gazed-and-gazed-but little thought
What wealth the show to me had brought:

THOMAS MOORE
1779-1852

In his time Tom Moore, the Dublin poet from Aungier Street, was as popular as Cliff Richard is today. Crowds at the theatre would rise to their feet on his arrival. At a dance a girl who shook hands with him afterwards covered her hands with her shawl. Even as far away as Niagara Falls a watchmaker refused to charge him for mending his watch. He was paid the equivalent today of a million pounds for his poem 'Lalla Rookh', and the poet Lord Byron considered himself flattered that Moore would consent to write his biography. Never in history perhaps has a poet been so popular in his lifetime. But wee Tommy had the advantage of not only being a poet but a singer as well, and his songs had become popular favourites such as 'Oft in the Stilly Night', 'The Minstrel Boy' and 'Believe Me if All those Endearing Young Charms'. A lot of his tunes came from Irish airs which Moore, like a good grocer's son, had jazzed up. But in what is considered his greatest poem he showed that he had a real understanding of the stressed rhythm of Gaelic poetry, which has a haunting echo that you can catch if you read it out loud. I think nothing in the work of his contemporaries Byron, Shelley or Wordsworth ever exceeded the pathos of this unique lament.

At the Mid Hour of the Night

At the mid hour of night, when stars are weeping,
    I fly,
To the lone vale we loved, when life shone warm in
    thine eye;
And I think oft, if spirits can steal from the regions
    of air
To revisit past scenes of delight, thou wilt come to
    me there
And tell me our love is remembered, even in the sky!

Then I sing the wild song 'twas once such pleasure
    to hear!
When our voices, commingling, breathed like one on
    the ear;
And as Echo far off through the vale my sad orison
    rolls,
I think, Oh my love! 'tis thy voice from the Kingdom
    of Souls
Faintly answering still the notes that once were so
    dear.

T.S. ELIOT
1888-1965

There was a bit of a shindy in poetic circles recently about T.S. Eliot's famous long poem *The Waste Land* which now seems to have been simply a whole lot of separate poems pasted together. I have always thought of it as a suspicious document ever since I read the poet Ezra Pound's edited version of it in which, with Eliot's permission, Pound struck out whole sections of the script, as a frenzied sub-editor might do, trying to get the latest edition of his evening paper to bed. Neither have I been able to share Eliot's fascination with the smells of steaks in passageways or his yen for yellow fog. Curiously enough where he really scores in my book, is in his poems about cats which he published in 1936. In fact, his greatest stage success in London or on Broadway was a musical put together about two adventurous pussy cats, Growltiger and Macavity. I saw it in New York along with the distinguished critic Denis Donoghue and we both went home in a state of high euphoria after being captivated by Eliot's magic theatrical treat.

from Macavity: The Mystery Cat

Macavity's a Mystery Cat: he's called the Hidden Paw –
For he's the master criminal who can defy the Law.
He's the bafflement of Scotland Yard, the
    Flying Squad's despair:
For when they reach the scene of crime – *Macavity's
    not there!*

Macavity, Macavity, there's no one like Macavity,
He's broken every human law, he breaks the law
    of gravity.
His powers of levitation would make a fakir stare,
And when you reach the scene of crime – *Macavity's
    not there!*
You may seek him in the basement, you may look
    up in the air –
But I tell you once and once again, *Macavity's not there!*

....

Macavity, Macavity, there's no one like Macavity,
There never was a Cat of such deceitfulness and
    suavity.
He always has an alibi, and one or two to spare:
At whatever time the deed took place –
    MACAVITY WASN'T THERE!
And they say that all the Cats whose wicked deeds
    are widely known
(I might mention Mungojerrie, I might mention
    Griddle-bone)
Are nothing more than agents for the Cat who all
    the time
Just controls their operations: the Napoleon of Crime!

WALTER PATER
1839-1894

'Mona Lisa', the first poem in W.B. Yeats's choice of modern verse for the *Oxford Book of Modern Verse*, actually started off as a piece of prose by Walter Pater about Leonardo da Vinci's painting. Yeats, with his uncanny ear for rhythm, was able to spot a poetic line running through Pater's prose and break it down into verse which catches something of the enigma of the famous smile. Of course, that literary cowboy Dan Brown has put his own gloss on the smile in order to make millions out of his dreadful novel *The Da Vinci Code*. Incredibly, he asks us to accept that the lady in the painting looking so pleased with herself is doing so because she knows (wink wink!) that Christ had a daughter with Mary Magdalen called Sarah. It's almost as ludicrous as claiming that the portrait of Lady Lavery by Orpen, which was reproduced on our bank notes, is Our Lady in disguise. Anything for a buck. Anyway, here is Walter Pater's 'Mona Lisa', rejigged by Yeats in the Oxford book, which says more in twenty lines than a single sentence in Brown's preposterous book.

Mona Lisa

She is older than the rocks among which she sits;
Like the Vampire,
She has been dead many times,
And learned the secrets of the grave;
And has been a diver in deep seas,
And keeps their fallen day about her;
And trafficked for strange webs with Eastern merchants;
And, as Leda,
Was the mother of Helen of Troy,
And, as St. Anne,
Was the mother of Mary;
And all this has been to her but as the sound of lyres and
    flutes,
And lives
Only in the delicacy
With which it has moulded the changing lineaments,
And tinged the eyelids and the hands.

ROBERT FROST
1874-1963

'A poem is never a put up job; it begins with a tug in the throat' wrote US poet Robert Frost. Frost used to let his mind write the poem without too much supervision, before polishing it and sending it on its way. He went on to become a major American poet, some people think even greater than Walt Whitman. There are two views about his work though – one that he is derivative and the other that he is one of the important poets of the twentieth century, a view shared by the writer.

Frost came to England for some years before the first world war and, encouraged by Rupert Brooke, established a reputation on both sides of the Atlantic. He reached the climax of his popularity in 1961 when he read his poem 'The Gift Outright' at President Kennedy's inauguration ceremony. I heard him read in the University College Dublin physics theatre in the 1950s and found him somewhat wooden, giving the impression that another man other than the author was reading the verse.

Stopping by Woods on a Snowy Evening

Whose woods these are I think I know.
His house is in the village, though;
He will not see me stopping here
To watch his woods fill up with snow.

My little horse must think it queer
To stop without a farmhouse near
Between the woods and frozen lake
The darkest evening of the year.

He gives his harness bells a shake
To ask if there is some mistake.
The only other sound's the sweep
Of easy wind and downy flake.

The woods are lovely, dark and deep,
But I have promises to keep,
And miles to go before I sleep,
And miles to go before I sleep.

SIEGFRIED SASSOON
1886-1967

Lieutenant Philip Sassoon was awarded the military cross for bravery in the Great War after being denied the Victoria Cross because of a clerical technicality. He didn't give a damn about decorations but cared a great deal about the injustice of the war he was fighting in. 'I am convinced that the war is being deliberately prolonged by those who have the power to end it', he told his commanding officer and in the same breath resigned from the army. This, of course, in those days, could mean execution by a firing squad.

Sassoon's father, Sir Philip, was one of the most powerful men in England and succeeded in placing Siegfried in Craiglockhart hospital in Edinburgh in order to rest up his nerves. In hospital he wrote *Counter Attack* which contains some of the most horrific poems ever written about war and which had a profound effect on the next generation in England. Siegfried Sassoon was known as 'Mad Jack' when he was in the army because of his habit of breaking into uncontrollable laughter at the pomposity of the drill he was meant to be giving his men. Curiously, his best prose book, a classic, *Memoirs of a Fox Hunting Man*, describes hunts in which he would have ridden with many of the purple-faced military types whom he satirised in this perfect little poem about the top brass in the army.

The General

'Good-morning; good-morning!' the General said
When we met him last week on our way to the line.
Now soldiers he smiled at are most of 'em dead,
And we' cursing his staff for incompetent swine.
'He's a cheery old card,' grunted Harry to Jack
As they slogged up to Arras with rifle and pack.

But he did for them both by his plan of attack.

ALFRED LORD TENNYSON
1809-1892

James Joyce, who liked nicknames, used to call Lord Tennyson Lawn Tennison. Though he could be prissy Tennyson was a real music maker in words. Poems like 'Morte d'Arthur', 'The Lotus Eaters' and 'Locksley Hall' run into the ear with the sparkle of spring water. However he also wrote drivel like 'Lady Clara Vere de Vere', which shows that a poet should never write to order, but only when an itch of the heart urges him to do so.

Tennyson's demeanour and patriarchal beard concealed a man of action (his son Lionel Tennyson was captain of England's cricket team) and he was cute enough to remain on the right side of Queen Victoria. As a young man W.B. Yeats was a great admirer of Tennyson and was much taken aback when the great French poet Paul Verlaine, far gone in drink, growled that Tennyson's famous poem about his dead friend Arthur Hallam, 'In Memoriam', was a fake. 'When Tennyson should have been broken hearted he had many memories.'

Here's how Tennyson, in perhaps his best known poem, sees Ulysses and his crew about to set out on their last voyage into the unknown.

from Ulysses

The lights begin to twinkle from the rocks;
The long day wanes; the slow moon climbs; the deep
Moans round with many voices. Come, my friends.
'Tis not too late to seek a newer world.
Push off, and sitting well in order smite
the sounding furrows; for my purpose holds
To sail beyond the sunset, and the baths
Of all the western stars, until I die.
It may be that the gulfs will wash us down;
It may be that we shall touch the Happy Isles,
And see the great Achilles, whom we knew.
Though much is taken, much abides; and though
We are not now that strength which in old days
Moved earth and heaven, that which we are, we are---
One equal temper of heroic hearts,
Made weak by time and fate, but strong in will
To strive, to seek, to find, and not to yield.

THOMAS MCDONAGH
1878-1916

Ninety-one years ago Thomas McDonagh was preparing for the Easter Rising of which he would be one of the leaders. The previous year he had organised the Howth gun running operation which had provided guns for the Rising. This extraordinary little man from Cloughjordan was a lecturer in English at University College Dublin and a poet who had written a seminal book on the influence of Anglo-Saxon stressed rhythm on Irish verse. A case could be made that his translation of 'The Yellow Bittern' from Irish into English is the most perfect of its kind, bringing from one language to another an orchestral arrangement of musical language that was unique in European verse. He had written a successful Abbey play, *When the Dawn is Come,* and married a beautiful girl from an Anglo-Irish family from Rathmines by whom he had two children.

But fair Ireland was all his cry. As a signatory to the proclamation and the commandant of the Jacob's factory in Bishop Street during the Rising he was among the sixteen executed in May 1916. A British officer who witnessed the event said, 'They all died well, but McDonagh died like a prince.'

from The Stars Stand Up in the Air

The stars stand up in the air,
The sun and the moon are gone,
The strand of its waters is bare,
And her sway is swept from the swan.

The cuckoo was calling all day,
Hid in the branches above,
How my stoirín is fled away,
'tis my grief that I gave her my love.

But sweeter than violin or lute
Is my love – and she left me behind.
I wish that all music were mute,
And I to all beauty were blind.

She's more shapely than swan by the strand,
She's more radiant than grass after dew,
She's more fair than the stars where they stand –
'tis my grief that her ever I knew!

(Translated from Irish by Thomas McDonagh)

PADRAIC COLUM
1881-1972

In 1967 Padraic Colum the poet asked me to the first night of his musical *Carricknabauna* featuring Art Carney which opened in New York. As he greeted members of the audience in the foyer some of them said, 'It is a pity your father didn't live to see this'. He had to explain that he was that father, the one who had been Yeats's favourite young poet and the author of the words of 'She Moves Through the Fair'. At eighty-six he looked like a young chap. He left Dublin in 1914 for the wrong reason – a pushy wife Molly who wanted to air her learning in New York academic circles. Before Padraic left Dublin he had written fine poetry and a notable play, *The Fiddler's House*, the first realist work at the Abbey. But he never improved on these until after his wife's death in 1961. He came back after that to Dublin each year and holed up in his sister Susan's house in Ranelagh where I used to visit him for a chuckle and a chat. The verse plays which he then wrote for the Lantern Theatre in Dublin sadly showed what he might have done in the intervening years had he not gone to the States.

I went to see him his a few months before he died near Deerfield, Massachusetts and found him chattering away like a cheerful robin avid for news of Dublin. He was chuffed to hear that his poem 'An Old Woman of the Roads' had been recited recently at a concert in Dublin, an indication that his early work might not be just for an age but for all time. Here it is.

An Old Woman of the Roads

Oh, to have a little house!
To own the hearth and stool and all!
The heaped-up sods upon the fire,
The pile of turf against the wall!

To have a clock with weights and chains
And pendulum swinging up and down,
A dresser filled with shining delph,
Speckled and white and blue and brown!

I could be busy all day
Clearing and sweeping hearth and floor,
And fixing on their shelf again
My white and blue and speckled store!

Och! But I'm weary of mist and dark,
And roads where there's never a house nor bush,
And tired I am of bog and road,
And the crying wind and the lonesome hush!

And I am praying to God on high,
And I am praying to him night and day,
For a little house, a house of my own -
Out of the wind's and the rain's way.

LADY DUFFERIN
1807-1867

A good follier up to 'Molly Malone' is 'O Bay of Dublin'. The first time I heard it was when Brendan Behan's mother Kathleen sang it for the American ambassador, Walter Curley, and his wife Taitsie, when we were having a drink in Bill Fuller's Old Sheiling pub looking down on Dublin Bay itself. What struck me about it was that it had two words in it to rhyme with 'Dublin' just like an Eminem rap. The poem was written by a Marchioness, Lady Dufferin, who was a descendent of Richard Brinsley Sheridan, the greatest playwright of the eighteenth century and whose famous play *The School for Scandal* is based on Dublin repartee.

from O Bay of Dublin

O Bay of Dublin! My heart you're troublin'
Your beauty haunts me like a fevered dream,
Like frozen fountains that the sun sets bubblin',
My heart's blood warms when I but hear your name.
And never till this life pulse ceases,
My earliest thoughts you'll cease to be;
O there's no one here knows how fair that place is,
And no one cares how dear it is to me.

Sweet Wicklow mountains! The sunlight sleeping
On your green banks is a picture rare;
You crowd around me like young girls peeping,
And puzzling me to say which is most fair;
As though you'd see your own sweet faces,
Reflected in that smooth and silver sea,
O! my blessing on those lovely places,
Though no one cares how dear they are to me.

GERARD MANLEY HOPKINS
1844-1889

I think that along with Shakespeare and Yeats, Gerard Manley Hopkins is the best poet the English language has produced though his output was small. For some reason the Jesuit fathers here don't make as much of him as they could, though he spent the second part of his life, an Englishman in exile, in a cold room at the top of the Jesuit College at 86 St. Stephen's Green, Dublin, where he was a lecturer. Neither did he mix with the literary set, though he only missed doing so by a whisker when one day he visited Yeats' father's studio at Number 3 St. Stephen's Green. The poetess Katherine Tynan had brought the shy Jesuit to meet Willie, but the young man had a fierce toothache which he was trying to kill with chloroform and had taken so much he had been asleep for two days. You can visit Gerard Manley Hopkins's grave today in Glasnevin cemetery where he is buried in the Jesuit communal grave.

I think my favourite Hopkins poem is 'Felix Randal', which tells of a dying blacksmith, whom Hopkins had attended during the last months of his illness. We see the man on his death bed stripped now of his powerful strength and are given a glimpse of him in his prime, massive muscles gleaming in the dim forge as he swings his hammer to shape the molten steel for the horse.

Read out loud, the last two lines evoke the crash of steel upon the anvil. Hopkins can infuse magic into the most ordinary words. Who, for instance, would dare use the word 'pining' twice and yet leave us with the image of a mighty man 'big boned and hardy-handsome'.

It not what you say, it's the way that you say it. By the way, the blacksmith's real name was Drayton not Randal.

Erratum

In the final line below the last
two words should read
"... battering sandal".

from Felix Randal

Felix Randal the farrier, O he is dead then? My duty all
  ended
Who watched his mould of man, big-boned and hardy-
  handsome
Pining, pining, till time when reason rambled in it and
  some
Fatal four disorders, fleshed there, all contended?

Sickness broke him. Impatient he cursed at first, but
  mended
Being anointed and all; though a heavenlier heart began
  some
Months earlier, since I had our sweet reprieve and
  ransom
Tendered to him. Ah well, God rest him all road ever he
  offended!

This seeing the sick endears them to us, us too it endears.
My tongue had taught thee comfort, touch had quenched
  thy tears,
Thy tears that touched my heart, child, Felix, poor Felix
  Randel;

How far from then forethought of, all thy more
  boisterous years,
When thou at the random grim forge, powerful amidst
  peers,
Didst fettle for the great grey drayhorse his bright and
  bettering sandal!

KUNO MEYER
1858-1919

Professor Kuno Meyer, strolling down Grafton Street in his light brown overcoat, large soft brown hat and flowing mustaches, had become a Dublin character in the first decade of the last century. You would have never thought that he was one of the leading German scholars of the day who had devoted his life to the study of early Irish poetry, which the lazy Irish had done little or nothing about. The leading novelist of the time, George Moore, who lived in Ely Place, used to say that Meyer's translations from the Irish were so good that 'we seem to see in them those early times, as in a mirror'.

Dublin thanked this marvellous man for his achievement by erasing his name from the role of honour in the City Hall in 1915 because Meyer had been so impertinent as to support his own country against England in the First World War. Ironically, Meyer admired his Anglo-Saxon cousins and was an ardent cricketer who rather fancied himself in his white flannels and blue belt when he played the game at Queens College, Liverpool. A bust of Kuno Meyer in Merrion Square would not be out of place to honour his memory. If it did nothing else it would do something to offset the gross representation of Oscar Wilde at the Lincoln Place side of the square, which to me evokes an image of the film actor Peter O'Toole sliding down a hill after a night on the razzle.

Here are three little jewels from ninth-century Irish verse (all of course by different poets), which Meyer has translated. The first one, 'The Pilgrim at Rome', is a cautionary note to over-zealous papal tourists.

The Pilgrim at Rome

To go to Rome
Is much of trouble, little of profit;
The King whom thou seekest here,
Unless thou bring Him with thee, thou wilt not find.

The Church Bell in the Night

Sweet little bell
That is struck in the windy night,
I prefer go to a tryst with thee
Than to a tryst with a foolish woman.

The Crucifixion

At the cry of the first bird
They began to crucify Thee, O cheek like a swan
It were not right ever to cease lamenting –
It was like the parting of day from night.

Ah! though sore the suffering
Put upon the body of Mary's Son –
Sorer to Him was the grief
That was upon her for His sake.

ALARIC ALEXANDER WATTS
1797-1864

Yeats's best-known poem, 'The Lake Isle of Innisfree', is famous for its evocation of the gurgle of water tripping over stones: 'I hear lake water lapping with low sounds by the shore.' This is largely achieved by three of the words in the line starting with the same letter, a device which is called by the arty folk 'alliteration'. Another example is Shakespeare's line where Macbeth says of his dead friend Duncan, 'after life's fitful fever he sleeps well.'

But only one practitioner has dared to write a poem of twenty-six lines with each line dedicated to a different letter of the alphabet, which is repeated throughout the line. This guy was Alaric Alexander Watts, one time private tutor to the family of the Prince Regent's dentist. Watts, a sturdy English gent with the rugged look of a front row forward, wrote loads of indifferent poetry, which was published in literary magazines of the time. But the only one which has lasted is 'An Austrian Army', perhaps because of its sheer effrontery.

This is some poem. If you said it out loud in a pub you could soon have everyone stamping their feet as if they were at Tom Barry's annual commemoration in Kilmichael. Maybe Watts was a better poet than he seemed. Lamb and Wordsworth were said to like his verse. He received a Civil List pension in 1869 from the Queen and 'fiddled and philosophised' til he died four years later.

NB: The word 'essay' in the fifth line is not intended to mean the chore one does at school, but is used in the context of 'to attempt or try', and is pronounced with the emphasis on the first syllable – ESS-ay.

from An Austrian Army

An Austrian army awfully array'd,
Boldly by battery besieged Belgrade.
Cossack commanders cannonading come
Dealing destruction's devastating doom:
Every endeavour engineers ess-ay,
For fame, for fortune fighting-furious fray!
Generals 'gainst generals grapple, gracious God!
How Heaven honours heroic hardihood!

..…   .….   …..…..   ..…   …..   …..

Unwise, unjust, unmerciful Ukraine!
Vanish, vain victory! Vanish, victory vain!
Why wish we warfare? Wherefore welcome were
Xerxes, Ximenes, Xanthus, Xavier?
Yield, yield, ye youths, ye yeomen, yield your yell:
Zeno's Zimmermann's, Zoroaster's zeal,

BRENDAN BEHAN
1923-1964

When I heard that a major oil strike might be made near the
Blasket Islands it occurred to me that I was in nearby Dunquin
in 1945 when the last person left the great Blasket. I knew
nothing then of its extraordinary history, how scholars from
all over Europe had felt themselves privileged to talk with the
inhabitants and write down their conversation and stories
which were older than Europe itself.

One man had his eye on the whole scene of desolation
however, a young Dubliner called Brendan Behan who had
just been released from prison for his IRA activities. He was to
write an exquisite poem which sums up the sadness of an Ire-
land which even at that time was not above selling its soul to
big business. The poem written in Irish is a little masterpiece,
as good as anything written by the poets of the Irish Literary
Renaissance, and even one might dare to say almost in the
class of the arch-poet Yeats himself. Here is my translation.

A Jackeen Says Goodbye to the Blaskets

The great sea under the setting sun gleams like a glass,
Not a sail in sight, no living person to see it pass
Save the last golden eagle, hung high on the edge of the
world,
Over the lonely Blasket resting, his wings unfurled.

Yes, the sun's at rest now and shadows thicken the light,
A rising moon gleams coldly through the night,
Stretching thin fingers down the quivering air,
On desolate, deserted dwellings, pitifully bare.

Silent save for birds' wings clipping the foam,
Heads on breast, they rest content, grateful to be home.
The wind lifts lightly, setting the half-door aslope
On a famished hearth without heat, without protection,
without hope.

(Translated by Ulick O'Connor)

PATRICK KAVANAGH
1905-1967

How many who looked at the bent figure hunched over a glass of whiskey in McDaids pub or The Bailey or Davy Byrnes engaged in serial diatribe realised that they were looking at Ireland's second best poet of the century?

I was thinking of him this autumn because October was the most important month for him. It was the one in which he could recharge his batteries and communicate best with the forces of nature which, he believed, drove his poetic output. No matter how low an ebb he had reached, he'd recharge himself this month for the contest of life. He drew power from the earth as a car refuels from a petrol pump.

By the way, guess when Paddy Kavanagh's birthday was – 21st October.

October

O Leafy yellowness you create for me
A world that was and now is poised above time,
I do not need to puzzle out Eternity
As I walk this arboreal street on the edge of a town.
The breeze too, even the temperature
And pattern of movement is precisely the same
As broke my heart for youth passing. Now I am sure
Of something. Something will be mine wherever I am.
I want to throw myself on the public street without
caring
For anything but the prayering that the earth offers.
It is October over all my life and the light is staring
As it caught me once in a plantation by the fox coverts.
A man is ploughing ground for winter wheat
And my nineteen years weight heavily on my feet.

ARTHUR CLOUGH
1819-1861

Arthur Hugh Clough, Matthew Arnold and John Ruskin were three Victorian writers who felt that poetry might be influential in creating a better way of life for the underprivileged. They were in fact the forbearers of the socialist regime which would come into power in England in 1945 under Clement Atlee and cleanse the system of some of its monstrosities. Though he was at one time principal of University Hall and a fellow of Oriel College Oxford, Clough used to describe himself as a republican and anti-capitalist. This led him to support George Sands, the French woman novelist who was regarded in her day as a type of female Satan. Ironically enough, Clough's best known poem 'Say Not the Struggle Nought Availeth', is probably sung more than any other hymn in churches throughout the Anglican community in England today. The last verse I hold to be among the finest in the language.

PS. The name Clough is pronounced Cluff as in wuff-wuff, bow-wow speak.

from Say Not the Struggle Nought Availeth

Say not the struggle nought availeth,
The labour and the wounds are vain,
The enemy faints not, nor faileth,
And as things have been they remain.

For while the tired waves, vainly breaking,
Seem here no painful inch to gain,
Far back, through creeks and inlets making,
Comes silent, flooding in, the main.

And not by eastern windows only,
Where daylight comes, comes in the light;
In front, the sun climbs slow, how slowly,
But westward look, the land is bright.

WILFRID GIBSON
1878-1962

Bet you never heard of Wilfrid Gibson. But he published hundreds of poems and was under the wing of the powerful poet protector, Edward Marsh (Churchill's wartime secretary), and was a friend of the famous poet Rupert Brooke. Yet no one picked up on his verse at the beginning of the month when they commemorated the ghastly carnage of the Somme. He refused a commission and served as a private soldier dedicating himself to helping the poor, which may have left him little time for high society chirrup. The nine lines below can make you break out in a cold sweat.

Breakfast

We ate our breakfast on our backs
Because the shells were screeching overhead.
I bet a rasher to a loaf of bread
That Hull United would beat Halifax
When Jimmy Sainthorpe played full-back instead
Of Billy Bradford. Ginger raised his head
And cursed, and took the bet, and dropt back dead.
We ate our breakfast lying on our backs
Because the shells were screeching overhead.

DOUGLAS HYDE
1856-1949

Last year was the one hundredth and fiftieth anniversary of the birth of Douglas Hyde, the first President of Ireland (1935-1949), who is buried in the graveyard of the Protestant Church Portahard near Frenchpark where his father was rector.

Douglas Hyde was the founder of the Gaelic League and inspired many of the writers of the Irish Literary Renaissance. His translations of Gaelic poetry opened a door for literary giants like Yeats, Synge and Lady Gregory to view the elements of a verse tradition unique in Europe. Hyde's ear for the music of words was such that he could turn the melodies and chimes of Gaelic verse back into English without losing the meaning of the original poem.

As a professor in University College Dublin Hyde taught my mother Celtic Studies. The students loved him because of his sense of fun. She used to recall how, on one occasion, at Christmas time they threw snowballs at him as he came through the gate of Earlsfort Terrace. Their professor simply tied his handkerchief to his umbrella and sailed through with his flag of truce.

Hyde had that rare gift of being able to write an almost perfect play. His *The Twisting of the Rope* was the first play in Irish presented in a professional theatre. Here is his translation of the lament of a young girl for her lost lover.

from Ringleted Youth of My Love
(from the Irish)

Ringleted youth of my love,
With thy locks bound loosely behind thee,
You passed by the road above,
But you never came in to find me;
Where were the harm for you
If you came for a little to see me,
Your kiss is wakening dew
Were I ever so ill or so dreamy.

I thought, O my love! You were so –
As the moon is, or sun on a fountain
And I thought after that you were snow,
The cold snow on top of the mountain;
And I thought after that, you were more
Like God's lamp shining to find me,
Or the bright star of knowledge before,
And the star of knowledge behind me.

COVENTRY PATMORE
1823-1896

The Victorians were never quite able to make out whether Coventry Patmore, the aristocratic poet, was writing love poems or simply sex verse. Cutely enough he called his work *Poems of Married Love* which made them acceptable on upper class bedside tables. When the going got hot he turned Catholic, made four pilgrimages a year to Lourdes, and asked to be buried in the garb of a Franciscan while maintaining a guerrilla war with the current Cardinal Archbishop. A formidable looking man with vast convex brows, bluish gray eyes and a wilful sensuous mouth, he is remembered today, one hundred and eleven years after his death, for a poem he wrote about his own little boy. It is sentimental, but is saved from banality by the poet's magic touch.

from **The Toys**

My little Son, who look'd from thoughtful eyes
And moved and spoke in quiet grown-up wise,
Having my law the seventh time disobey'd
I struck him, and dismiss'd
With hard words and unkiss'd,
His Mother, who was patient, being dead.
Then, fearing lest his grief should hinder sleep,
I visited his bed,
But found him slumbering deep,
With darken'd eyelids, and their lashes yet
From his late sobbing wet.
And I alone,
Kissing away his tears, left others of my own;
For, on a table drawn beside his head,
He put, within his reach,
A box of counters and a red-vein'd stone,
A piece of glass abraded by the beach
To comfort his sad heart.

....

So when that night I pray'd
To God, I wept, and said
Ah, when at last we lie with drawn breath,
Not vexing Thee in death,
And Thou rememberest of what toys
We made our joys,
How weakly understood
Thy great commanded good,
Then, fatherly not less
Than I whom Thou hast moulded from the clay,
Thou'lt leave Thy wrath, and say,
'I will be sorry for their childishness.'

D.H. LAWRENCE
1885-1930

It's hard to believe that forty-five years ago a London book-seller who sold D.H. Lawrence's *Lady Chatterley's Lover* could have been put in the slammer for five years. It was banned everywhere as pornography. Today you can get the book in any Dublin bookshop without a bother.

Though Lawrence is now regarded as being amongst the best writers in English of the twentieth century, Evelyn Waugh didn't think so, dismissing him with a spiteful snarl, 'He couldn't write for toffee'.

If you want to try him begin with *Sons and Lovers*, the story of the coalmining family he grew up in, which portrays the heroism of motherhood as no one else has done. He was also a fine painter, playwright and magnificent poet. Here is one of his poems that make me shriek with laughter every time I read it.

Intimates

Don't you care for my love? she said bitterly

I handed her the mirror, and said:
Please address these questions to the proper person!
Please make all requests to headquarters!
In all matters of emotional importance
please approach the supreme authority direct!—

So I handed her the mirror.
And she would have broken it over my head,
but she caught sight of her own reflection
and that held her spellbound for two seconds
while I fled.

JAMES STEPHENS
1883-1950

Michael Collins was a believer in *dúireas*, which is the Irish word for good blood. It means if you come out of a good stable the cut of your jib is likely to show. For historical reasons breeding in Ireland had gone topsy-turvy and you might find a fellow in a cabin with the profile of a Florentine prince, or an old woman in a cottage with the elaborate courtesy of a Contessa.

James Stephens perfectly captures this dilemma in his poem 'Blue Blood'. The lads in the pub are all wondering if the stranger who has come among them is of chieftain stock or just a bowsy like the rest of them. Stephens himself, a tiny Dublin working-class Protestant, would become a legend in England for his brilliant talk in high society salons and his reciting of poetry on the BBC.

Blue Blood

We thought at first, this man is a king for sure,
Or the branch of a mighty and ancient and famous
  lineage
-That silly, sulky, illiterate, black-avised boor
Who was hatched by foreign vulgarity under a hedge!

The good men of Clare were drinking his health
  in a flood,
And gazing, with me, in awe at the princely lad;
And asking each other from what bluest blueness
  of blood
His daddy was squeezed, and the pa of the da of
  his dad?

We waited there, gaping and wondering, anxiously,
Until he'd stop eating, and let the glad tidings out;
And the slack-jawed booby proved to the hilt that he
Was lout, son of lout, by old lout, and was da to a lout!

W.B. Yeats
1865-1939

In Sligo awhile ago (to give a talk to the Yeats Society for the Yeats International Summer School), three pretty girls fully made up with fashionable bare navels asked me would I do them a favour. They wanted me to go and buy cigarettes for them in the shop I was going into. They were thirteen years of age. A far cry indeed from the youth of a man I was in Sligo to speak about.

The town is booming, tanning centres (for humans not cattle), beauty parlours, multiple hair stylists and shops of the calibre of Brown Thomas (Dublin) in the McGuire era. Yeats came from Sligo merchants on his mother's side and could not but have rejoiced in the town's present affluence ('My proudest boast', he used say, 'is that I can read a balance sheet at a glance').

But despite the festival and the fine Yeats Memorial Building there is not much evidence that Sligo is developing on the lines of a Florence of the North. The Hawk's Well theatre is closing down and the Blue Raincoat Theatre (state subsidised) took almost a year to deal with a play I sent them. Walking round the harbour there where ships owned by Yeats's Middleton uncles used to embark, I thought of the two things that had driven this amazing man: his ability to see beauty in simple things and his fanatic energy in casting it into verse. There is not one word in the poem below (written to his beloved Maud Gonne) that isn't of the most ordinary kind, yet they have been disposed in such a way so as to leave the reader with a glow in his mind after he has read it.

He Wishes for the Cloths of Heaven

Had I the heavens' embroidered cloths,
Enwrought with golden and silver light,
The blue and the dim and the dark cloths
Of night and light and the half-light,
I would spread the cloths under your feet:
But I, being poor, have only my dreams;
I have spread my dreams under your feet;
Tread softly because you tread on my dreams.

PATRICK PEARSE
1879-1916

A while ago you couldn't open your mouth in praise of Patrick Pearse without having nasty people shouting 'vampire, pervert'. Though Pearse had a bad press, mainly because of the innate Irish instinct for pulling any man down who has tried to help them (as exemplified by Parnell's downfall), it was left to a former editor of *The London Times*, Lord Rees-Mogg, to eulogise him three years ago and point out that Pearse's published ideas as a schoolmaster on teaching were 'one hundred years before their time'.

These days, however, An Piarsach appears to be coming into his own. His last letter from his cell in Kilmainham jail sold for one hundred thousand euro at the Adams and Mealy auction. Many a time one has looked at the fine head of Pearse, which faces St. Enda's Pearse Museum in Rathfarnham, and wondered will we ever give proper recognition to one of our greatest of Irishmen? Not that Pearse would give a damn about recognition; but he would have had a sense of fulfilment about what is happening in the North where Irishmen of both traditions are now joining together to rule.

St. Enda's School, which has been made into a museum, houses brilliant sculptures by Pearse's brother Willie. The two were as close as Siamese twins and talked to each other in a sort of jargon of their own. Willie in his cell in Kilmainham, awaiting his own execution (scarcely justified by his lowly military role), must have heard the shots that finished off his brother in the courtyard down below. We have a glimpse of how the two brothers felt about one another from a haunting poem, which Patrick wrote to Willie after Willie had gone to Paris to study art.

from The Strand in Howth

Here in Ireland,
Am I, my brother,
And you far from me
In gallant Paris,

I beholding
Hill and harbour,
The strand of Howth
And Slieverua's side,

And you victorious
In mighty Paris
Of the limewhite palaces
And the surging hosts;

And what I ask
Of you, beloved,
Far away
Is to think at times

Of the corncrake's tune
Beside Glasnevin
In the middle of the meadow
Speaking in the night;

Of the voice of the birds
In Glenasmole
Happily, with melody,
Chanting music.

JOHN BETJEMAN
1906-1984

The year 2006 was the one hundredth anniversary of John Bet-
jeman's birth. Because he wrote in rhyme and rhythm and
about things in every day life Betjeman was sneered at by the
iron guard of academic criticism in his time. But his verse sur-
vives today stronger than ever. He had a break in 1941 when
he was sent to Éire as an attaché to the United Kingdom Min-
ister. Neutral Dublin was awash with not only good food, but
good writers and artists as well – the likes of Frank O'Connor,
Sean O'Faolain, Myles Na gCopaleen, Valentine Iremonger,
Patrick Kavanagh, Lord Dunsany and Micheal McLiammoir.
In painting there was Jack Yeats, Sean Keating and Paul
Henry. Betjeman made himself immensely helpful to these
artists in making their work known in London. (He also
helped with a survey of architecture for the tourist board and
lured film directors like Laurence Olivier to Ireland to make
the famous movie *Henry V* at Powerscourt).

Of course, Sean O'Betjeman as he called himself wasn't
just over here to encourage Irish art. In Portmarnock Golf
Club, where he was a popular member, members still
swapped tales of how 'Betchers' kept an open ear for even the
most outrageous snippets of current Irish life they would re-
tail to him. If he wasn't all that good as a spy he was an im-
mense success in keeping the relations between our two coun-
tries at top level. As Frank Gallagher, the director of the Irish
Government Information Service said, 'John found something
to hurroosh for in all of us'. Here is how this very English
Englishman saw us Irish.

174

from Ireland with Emily

Bells are booming down the bohreens
White the mist along the grass.
Now the Julias, Maeves and Maureens
Move between the fields to Mass.
Twisted trees of small green apple
Guard the decent whitewashed chapel,
Gilded gates and doorway grained
Pointed windows richly stained
With many-coloured Munich glass.

See the black-shawled congregations
On the broidered vestment gaze
Murmur past the painted stations
As Thy Sacred Heart displays
Lush Kildare of scented meadows,
Roscommon, thin in ash-tree shadows,
And Westmeath the lake-reflected,
Spreading Leix the hill-protected,
Kneeling all in silver haze?

...   .

Stony seaboard, far and foreign,
Stony hills poured over space,
Stony outcrop of the Burren,
Stones in every fertile place,
Little fields with boulders dotted,
Grey-stone shoulders saffron-spotted,
Stone-walled cabins thatched with reeds,
Where a Stone Age people breeds
The last of Europe's stone age race.

DYLAN THOMAS
1914-1953

It took Dylan Thomas, the Welsh poet, two hundred drafts of his most famous poem 'Fern Hill' before he felt he had got it right. In the end he took so long that it arrived at the printers too late to be included in his poetry collection published Christmas 1946. When he refused to let the book go out unless they included this poem they managed to squeeze it in as the last poem in the book.

Thomas used language like the Impressionist painters used paint, making one word suggest a number of other things. For instance, in the first verse of 'Fern Hill' 'the lilting house' doesn't mean that the house itself lilts but that it re-sounds with the music of the birds and the wind around it. Then just below, 'Honoured among the wagons I was prince of the apple towns' brings before the mind a vivid image of a boy on top of a hay cart passing through an apple grove.

Of course, most of the critics of the time failed to catch the flavour of Thomas' innovations, but he didn't give a tinker's damn and dismissed them simply as 'Men who speak as though they had the Elgin marbles in their mouths'.

from Fern Hill

Now as I was young and easy under the apple boughs
About the lilting house and happy as the grass was
  green,
The night above the dingle starry,
Time let me hail and climb
Golden in the heydays of his eyes,
And honoured among the wagons I was prince of
  the apple towns,
And once below a time I lordly had the trees and leaves
Trail with daisies and barley
Down the rivers of the windfall light.
....

Nothing I cared, in the lamb white days, that time would
  take me,
Up to the swallow thronged loft by the shadow of
  my hand,
In the moon that is always rising,
Nor that riding to sleep
I should hear him fly with the high fields
And wake to the farm forever fled from the
  childless land.
Oh as I was young and easy in the mercy of his means,
Time held me green and dying
Though I sang in my chains like the sea.

DENNY LANE
1818-1895

Denny Lane is remembered for the song he wrote, 'Carrigdhoun', which is still a favourite at ballad sessions today. It deals with the hundreds of thousands of young Irishman who, after the Battle of the Boyne, rather than fight under Orange Billy took off for France to wear the fleur-de-lis in the army of the Catholic monarch there. 'Carrigdhoun' is a beautifully woven song and the words have almost as much music in them if you just read them as when they are sung to music.

Denny Lane was an extraordinary all rounder. A Trinity student from Cork, along with Thomas Davis and John Blake Dillon they founded the famous paper *The Nation* which quickly found itself with a circulation of twice any other Irish paper. It had huge influence and was a mouthpiece for the Young Irelanders who planned the 1848 Rising. Lane was arrested then but went on to become one of the most successful men in Munster and director of the Cork Gas Company.

In 2003 his papers were discovered in the attic of a house owned by his grandson. When they are properly researched Denny Lane's name may well figure, along with Thomas Davis, William Smith O'Brien and Charles Gavan Duffy, as a key figure in the struggle for Irish freedom.

from Carrigdhoun

On Carrigdhoun the heath is brown,
The clouds are dark over Ardnalee,
And many a stream comes rushing down
To swell the angry Owenabwee.
The moaning blast is sweeping fast
Thru' many a leafless tree,
And I'm alone, for he is gone,
My hawk is flown, ochone machree!

Soft April showers and bright May flowers
Will bring the summer back again;
But will they bring me back the hours
I spent with my brave Domhnal then?
'Tis but a chance, for he's gone to France
To wear the fleur-de-lis;
But I'll follow you, my Domhnal dhu,
For still I'm true to you, a chroidhe

F.R. HIGGINS
1896-1941

Fred Higgins, an active socialist and founder of the Clerical Workers Union, somewhat surprisingly came from an ascendancy background and had been brought up at Higginstown House in County Meath. He would become one of the finest poets in English of the century. Yeats recognised this when he included six of Higgins' poems in the *Oxford Book of Modern Verse*. No other Irish poet has caught so well the exquisite halt of Gaelic metres and used it to seam the rhythmic pattern of his poems.

Here is a Higgins piece which tells of an encounter with a traveller, Hare-foot Mike, who presents the poet with a pair of musical clappers which he claims have come from the spine of Jezebel. Can't you catch the clack of the bones under the lines as the poet tips us his fancy tale?

Song for the Clatter-Bones

God rest that Jewish woman,
Queen Jezebel, the bitch
Who peeled the clothes from her shoulder-bones
Down to her spent teats
As she stretched out of the window
Among the geraniums, where
She chaffed and laughed like one half daft
Titivating her painted hair-

King Jehu he drove to her,
She tipped him a fancy beck;
But he from his knacky side-car spoke,
'Who'll break that dewlapped neck?'
And so she was thrown from the window;
Like Lucifer she fell
Beneath the feet of the horses and they beat
The light out of Jezebel.

That corpse wasn't planted in clover;
Ah, nothing of her was found
Save those grey bones that Hare-foot Mike
Gave me for their lovely sound;
And as once her dancing body
Made star-lit princes sweat,
So I'll just clack: though her ghost lacks a back
There's music in the old bones yet.

WILLIAM SHAKESPEARE
1564-1616

Some hold Macbeth's speech after his wife's death as Shakespeare's greatest from his thirty-eight plays. The word 'tomorrow' for instance is in itself not particularly exciting, but repeated here encased in the rhythmic cadence of the poet's sounding box it can suggest an agony of eternity which is sustained to the end of the sentence. Now a new sound takes over, the guttering cough of death in the line 'Out, out, brief candle!' The final stroll into the dark dismisses life as 'signifying nothing'. These lines in *Macbeth* would 400 years later thrill Samuel Beckett who has left us his take on the matter in *Waiting for Godot*:

> 'They give birth astride of a grave, the light gleams an
>   instant,
> then it's night once more.'

from Macbeth

To-morrow, and to-morrow, and to-morrow
Creeps in this petty pace from day to day,
To the last syllable of recorded time;
And all our yesterdays have lighted fools
The way to dusty death. Out, out, brief candle!
Life's but a walking shadow, a poor player
That struts and frets his hour upon the stage,
And then is heard no more. It is a tale
Told by an idiot, full of sound and fury,
Signifying nothing.

Æ
George Russell
1867-1935

Dublin's Rathgar must have something in it to catch an artist's eye. Joyce was born there (Brighton Square), as was John Synge (Orwell Park) and Yeats grew up just round the corner in Harold's Cross. On 17 Rathgar Avenue lived one of the princes of the Irish Literary Renaissance, George Russell (Æ). You can see his house with an enormous plaque commemorating him on the left hand side about half way down the avenue opposite the red brick national school. Here on Saturday evenings young writers used to come and partake in the poet-fest provided by Æ and his friends. George Moore, the outstanding living novelist in English at the time, used to attend and has described the scene as follows: 'Here at Russell's, is the mind of Corot the French painter in verse and prose; the happiness of a memorial moments under blossoming boughs when the soul rises to the lips.'

This decent man was a good enough poet to have three entries in the *Oxford Book of English Verse* which secures his reputation for posterity.

When

When mine hour is come
Let no teardrop fall
And no darkness hover
Round me where I lie.
Let the vastness call
One who was its lover,
Let me breathe the sky.

Where the lordly light
Walks along the world,
And its silent tread
Leaves the grasses bright,
Leaves the flowers uncurled,
Let me to the dead
Breathe a gay goodnight.

ROY CAMPBELL
1901-1957

Roy Campbell was one of the most famous poets of his time, ranked up along with Dylan Thomas, Edith Sitwell and admired by T.S. Eliot. This is the fiftieth anniversary of his death but there has been hardly a squeak in the papers about him. The left-wing press tried to wipe him out as a poet in his lifetime without success. But now that he is dead it seems they have succeeded. The image his enemies presented of Campbell was of a right-wing street basher. This despite the fact that he had fought the Nazis during the Second World War and ended up with a permanently injured leg. Campbell was in fact a forerunner of Brendan Behan and had the same ability to hit the headlines with outrageous remarks and loutish antics, as Brendan would do later on. It seemed untypical for a South African of Scots descent to behave like this. The truth was he was really an Irish South African whose ancestors came from Donegal. When I visited Campbell's nephew ten years ago I knocked on the door of the house, which was named 'Carndonagh' by their great grandfather who came from that Ulster town.

For sheer word music Campbell must rank as one of the best poets of the century, in that area alone in Yeats's class. Here is a poem of his about zebras that literally zings off the page so that you can see the striped animals running across the veldt in front of you as you read the singing lines. Don't miss that marvellous rhyme in the last four lines of 'fillies' and 'lilies', evoking the delicate trot of those ferociously fast beasts.

186

The Zebras

From the dark woods that breathe of fallen showers,
Harnessed with level rays in golden reins,
The zebras draw the dawn across the plains
Wading knee-deep among the scarlet flowers.
The sunlight, zithering their flanks with fire,
Flashes between the shadows as they pass
Barred with electric tremors through the grass
Like wind along the gold strings of a lyre.

Into the flushed air snorting rosy plumes
That smoulder round their feet in drifting fumes,
With dove-like voices call the distant fillies,
While round the herds the stallion wheels his flight,
Engine of beauty volted with delight,
To roll his mare among the trampled lilies.

AUSTIN CLARKE
1896-1974

Who was Dr. Kathleen Lynn? Well she was an important figure in the Easter Rising, the anniversary of which we celebrated last year. Why do we hear so little about her? Is it because she was a woman? Austin Clarke the poet seems to think so.

During the 1916 Rebellion Dr. Lynn, as a senior officer of the Citizen Army, negotiated the surrender of City Hall to the British. Later, when the New State was up and running she founded St. Ultans Hospital, the first one in Ireland devoted exclusively to the treatment of infants. With her friend Charlotte Ffrench-Mullen she would devote the rest of her life to this magnificent institution in Charlemont Street. Among the rash of statues of escaped rabbits and toy department Molly Malones which our City Council seem to regard as public statuary, a commemorative bust of Dr. Kathleen Lynn would not be out of place

Kathleen, a rector's daughter from Cong, County Mayo, was educated at Alexandra College and was a Fellow of the Royal College of Surgeons in Ireland. Though not cast in stone, Kathleen Lynn has been commemorated in verse by Austin Clarke in his poem 'The Subjection of Women'.

from The Subjection of Women

Few praise
Now Dr Kathleen Lynn, who founded
A hospital for sick babes, foundlings,
Saved them with lay hands. How could we
Look down on infants, prattling, cooing,
When wealth had emptied so many cradles?
Better than ours, her simple Credo.

Women, who cast off all we want,
Are now despised, their names unwanted,
For patriots in party statement
And act make worse our Ill-fare State.
The soul is profit. Money claims us.
Heroes are valuable clay.

W.B. YEATS

1865-1939

We are being constantly informed that it won't be long before
the world has used up its oil supply. Climate change rings a
knell of doom in the ears of scientists. Ice caps melt. Great cit-
ies like New Orleans are nearly demolished. Are we at the
edge of an apocalypse?

As early as January 1919 our national poet, W.B. Yeats,
sensed something was wrong in the works. He felt that spiri-
tual force was running out as it had done at the time of the
decline of the Roman Empire. Another revival was needed
like the one which followed the birth of Christ.

That is what his prophetic poem 'The Second Coming'
may be about, the vision of one who knows that mankind has
played around too much, and that material wealth can con-
sume the consumer. Once more we must 'live within the spir-
its fire'.

The Second Coming

Turning and turning in the widening gyre
The falcon cannot hear the falconer;
Things fall apart; the centre cannot hold;
Mere anarchy is loosed upon the world,
The blood-dimmed tide is loosed, and everywhere
The ceremony of innocence is drowned;
The best lack all conviction, while the worst
Are full of passionate intensity.

Surely some revelation is at hand;
Surely the Second Coming is at hand.
The Second Coming! Hardly are those words out
When a vast image out of Spiritus Mundi
Troubles my sight: somewhere in sands of the desert
A shape with lion body and the head of a man,
A gaze blank and pitiless as the sun,
Is moving its slow thighs, while all about it
Reel shadows of the indignant desert birds.
The darkness drops again; but now I know
That twenty centuries of stony sleep
Were vexed to nightmare by a rocking cradle,
And what rough beast, its hour come round at last,
Slouches towards Bethlehem to be born?

COPYRIGHT PERMISSIONS